THE COMPLETE
BAKING
AIR FRYER
COOKBOOK

THE COMPLETE
BAKING
AIR FRYER
COOKBOOK

75 baking recipes perfect for your air fryer

CONTENTS

A GUIDE TO
AIR FRYERS

TYPES OF AIR FRYER

The recipes in this book are based on an air fryer with a 6-quart capacity basket, which will fit a standard 8in (20cm) pan or ovenproof dish. Where a pan isn't required, you can bake in any size air fryer (the size of the basket will just affect the number of batches needed to cook the full recipe). If your air fryer has a small capacity, you can halve the recipe to accommodate a smaller pan; as a general rule, reduce the baking time by one-third, then check the bake.

HOW AIR FRYERS WORK

Air fryers have an electrical element at the top and a fan that pushes the heat around a basket, in which the food sits. Place what you are baking on the rack provided, as this allows heat to circulate underneath it. Often a dish may look cooked and brown on top but still need time to cook through from underneath where the heat is more gentle. Flipping is recommended for some food, while some are cooked at a higher heat initially to ensure it rises and colors, before decreasing the temperature to ensure thorough cooking.

SETTINGS

Most air fryers have multiple cooking settings. Use the bake setting unless the recipe states otherwise. Temperatures are the same as they would be if you were baking in a conventional oven, but some things will cook more quickly, especially if they have a high fat content. Dense bakes, such as loaf cakes, however, take a similar amount of time. As an air fryer can heat up within minutes, this dramatically reduces energy usage and makes for a very convenient way to bake. The reheat setting is great for warming food just before serving.

BAKING IN A PAN

Consider the size of your air fryer before buying pans to fit. You can use all ovenproof dishes. Metal pans conduct heat quickly and retain that heat so are good for getting a golden, crisp crust. Silicone is great for dishes that need a nonstick surface. If a recipe says to grease a pan, you can use soft butter, oil, or an oil spray. If the recipe also advises lining, cut a piece of parchment paper to the size of the base, then another for the sides. Trim any excess as it may catch on the element or blow around and damage your bake. Don't place parchment paper in the basket without anything to hold it down. It will blow into the heating element and cause a fire.

BAKING DIRECTLY IN THE BASKET

Some recipes require you place the food directly into the air fryer basket. Make sure you have the rack in the basket to allow the air to circulate for even baking. All air fryer racks have a nonstick coating, but giving them a light spray with oil can help ensure no sticking. Some recipes, such as cookies, call for the basket to be lined to prevent them from melting through the gaps. Cut a piece of parchment paper to the width of the rack, and fold any excess under to prevent the paper from being blown about during baking.

REMOVING BAKES FROM THE BASKET

Wearing oven mitts is the safest way to remove anything from most air fryers. There are also many dishes that need to cool and set, such as cookies or pastries. The easiest way to do this without any casualties is to remove the basket from the fryer and set it on a wire rack to cool. Once cooled to room temperature, use a spatula or your hands to gently lift them out.

BAKING IN BATCHES

Some recipes, such as cookies, will require baking in batches due to the lack of space in the air fryer. They take up a lot of surface area and need to be spaced out while baking to stop them from sticking to one another. Cookies, biscuits, and pastry are always best chilled before baking because of their high fat content, so it is best to store batches in the fridge until you're ready to bake them.

FREEZING

As a general rule, all cookies, biscuits, and pastries can be frozen while raw. This is super handy if you want to make a recipe, but don't want the full quantity at once, or want to prepare ahead for the future. Open-freeze cookies or pastries on a lined baking sheet, then transfer to an airtight container (this prevents them from sticking together). To bake from frozen, increase the time slightly and keep checking until cooked. Alternatively, leave to thaw at room temperature and bake as the recipe suggests.

5 BEST BAKES TO COOK IN THE AIR FRYER

1 GOOEY BROWNIES

2 SWEET AND SAVORY PASTRIES

3 COOKIES

4 MUFFINS AND CAKES

5 SWEET BUNS

BREAKFAST BAKES

Whether you opt for a sweet Danish, muffin, or pancake with your morning coffee or a nourishing savory morsel, this chapter is full of simple breakfast ideas for your air fryer, as well as lots of options for making ahead to fill your freezer ready for those busy mornings.

BANANA & COFFEE MUFFINS

¾ cup (180g) plain yogurt
⅔ cup (140ml) vegetable oil
2 eggs
¾ cup (150g) light brown sugar
3 small ripe bananas, mashed with
   some chunks left
1 tsp instant espresso
¾ cup (75g) pecan halves,
   roughly chopped
1 cup plus 2 tbsp (150g) all-purpose
   flour
2 tsp baking powder
1 cup plus 2 tbsp (150g) whole
   wheat flour
1 tbsp instant coffee powder
½ tsp salt

CRUMBLE TOPPING:
4 tbsp (60g) salted butter,
   cold and cubed
⅓ cup (50g) all-purpose flour
2 tbsp (25g) brown sugar
¼ cup (25g) pecan halves,
   roughly chopped
1 tsp instant coffee powder

1 Start by making the crumble topping. Place the cubed butter in a bowl with the flour, and rub between your fingers until you have a chunky crumble. Add the sugar, chopped pecans, and instant coffee powder. Set aside.

2 Combine the yogurt, oil, eggs, and sugar in a large bowl, and whisk until the sugar has dissolved. Add the mashed bananas, instant espresso, and chopped pecans, and fold through the mix. Sift the remaining dry ingredients into the bowl and fold again until everything is fully incorporated.

3 Preheat the air fryer to 325°F for 3 minutes.

4 Place 12 silicone muffin cases directly into the air fryer basket (or work in batches if needed), then fill each case about four-fifths full with batter.

5 Top generously with the crumble mixture.

6 Bake at 325°F for 25 minutes, then let cool on a wire rack.

KEEP IT Store for up to 5 days in an airtight container or freeze for up to 6 weeks.

**Prep + cook time
40 minutes
Makes 12**

PISTACHIO PAIN AU RAISIN

⅔ cup (100g) raisins, soaked in
   boiling water
1 x 11oz (320g) sheet of puff pastry
¾ cup (100g) pistachios, finely
   chopped
1 egg, beaten
⅓ cup (100g) apricot jam

PASTRY CREAM:
2 egg yolks
2 tbsp cornstarch
¼ cup (50g) sugar
1 tsp vanilla extract
1 cup (200ml) milk

1 For the pastry cream, whisk the yolks, cornstarch, sugar, and vanilla in a large heatproof bowl until the mixture is smooth.

2 Heat the milk in a wide saucepan over medium heat until starting to steam. Pour one-third of the milk into the yolk mixture, and whisk until combined. Stir in the rest of the hot milk and pour everything back into the pan over the heat.

3 Whisk the custard until it thickens, then remove from heat and beat well.

4 Pour the custard onto a clean baking sheet, and cover with plastic wrap to prevent a skin from forming. Let cool.

5 Drain the soaked raisins well in a strainer. Set aside.

6 Unroll the pastry, keeping it on the paper. Spread the cooled pastry cream evenly over the pastry.

7 Sprinkle with the raisins and three-quarters of the pistachios.

8 Using the edge of the parchment paper, roll the pastry tightly into a swirl from one of the short ends. Wrap in the paper and chill for 30 minutes.

9 Preheat the air fryer to 325°F for 3 minutes and line the basket with parchment paper.

10 Cut the roll into eight pieces, place on a parchment paper–lined baking sheet, and brush with egg. Cook in batches (keep other pastries in the fridge) in the lined air fryer basket for 25 minutes at 325°F. Cool on a wire rack.

11 Heat the apricot jam for 30 seconds in a microwave until melted, then brush it over the pastries. Top with the remaining pistachios.

KEEP IT Best eaten fresh, but will keep for 2 days in an airtight container. Reheat for 2 minutes in the air fryer.

**Prep + cook time
40 minutes, plus chilling
Makes 8**

MAPLE SYRUP PANCAKES

1½ cups (200g) all-purpose flour
½ tsp baking powder
½ tsp baking soda
¼ tsp fine salt
1 egg
¼ cup (60ml) maple syrup
1½ cups (300g) plain yogurt or kefir
2 tbsp (20g) butter, melted
to serve: Greek yogurt, berries,
   and maple syrup

1 Combine all the dry ingredients in a large mixing bowl. Whisk the egg, maple syrup, and yogurt in another. Pour the combined wet ingredients into the dry ingredients, and whisk until you have a smooth batter. Stir in the melted butter, and let the batter rest for 10 minutes or up to 1 hour.
2 Preheat the air fryer to 350°F for 3 minutes.
3 Fill 10 greased 4in (10cm) ramekins roughly ½in (1cm) deep with pancake batter, then place in the air fryer basket and bake for 5 minutes at 350°F (you may need to do this in batches).

4 Remove the pancakes from the ramekins, flip them over, and return to the fryer basket (on their own) for another 3 minutes.
5 Once all your pancakes are baked, stack them up and serve with yogurt, berries, and maple syrup.

**Prep + cook time
30 minutes
Makes 10**

OATY BLUEBERRY MUFFINS

1 cup (200g) plain yogurt
⅔ cup (140ml) vegetable oil
3 tbsp (45ml) maple syrup
2 eggs
½ cup (100g) light brown sugar,
    plus 1 tbsp for topping
1½ cups (200g) all-purpose flour
½ cup (50g) old-fashioned oats, plus
    2 tbsp for topping
1 tsp ground cinnamon
1½ tsp baking powder
¾ tsp salt
1¼ cups (150g) fresh blueberries or
    ¾ cup (150g) frozen blueberries
2 tbsp pumpkin seeds, plus 2 tbsp
    for topping

1 Combine the yogurt, oil, maple syrup, and eggs with the sugar in a bowl, and whisk until the sugar dissolves.
2 Add the flour, oats, cinnamon, baking powder, and salt, and mix until fully incorporated. Fold in the blueberries and pumpkin seeds.
3 Make the topping by mixing 1 tablespoon brown sugar with 2 tablespoons oats and 2 tablespoons pumpkin seeds in a bowl.
4 Preheat the air fryer to 325°F for 3 minutes.
5 Place 8 silicone muffin cases (lined with paper, if you like) directly into the air fryer basket (or work in batches if needed), then fill each case about four-fifths full with batter.
6 Sprinkle with the crunchy topping.
7 Bake at 325°F for 25 minutes, then let cool on a wire rack.

KEEP IT Store for up to 5 days in an airtight container, or freeze for up to 6 weeks.

Prep + cook time
40 minutes
Makes 8

APRICOT & ALMOND DANISHES

1 x 15oz (400g) can apricot halves
1 x 11oz (320g) sheet of puff pastry
1 tbsp milk
⅓ cup (30g) slivered almonds
½ cup (150g) apricot jam
to serve: powdered sugar

FRANGIPANE:
4 tbsp (60g) salted butter, softened
¼ cup (50g) sugar
¾ cup (80g) ground almonds
1 egg
1 tsp vanilla extract
3 tbsp (25g) all-purpose flour

TIP Heat the pastries for 1 minute at 325°F before serving for that just-baked warm taste!

1 Start by making the frangipane. In a mixing bowl, beat the butter and sugar with a wooden spoon for 3–5 minutes. Add the almonds, egg, and vanilla, and stir until combined. Fold in the flour. Set aside.

2 Drain the apricots and discard the syrup. Slice each apricot half into thirds; set aside.

3 Unroll the sheet of puff pastry and cut it into six 4in (10cm) squares (or a size to suit your air fryer).

4 Score a ¾in (2cm) border around the edge of each square, then place one-sixth of the frangipane in the center of each square. Gently spread the mixture out to fill the inner square.

5 Place the sliced apricots in rows on top of the frangipane. Nestle them close to each other, as they will shrink when baking.

6 Preheat the air fryer to 400°F for 3 minutes.

7 Brush each pastry edge with milk.

8 Using a spatula, place 2–4 pastries in the air fryer basket. Bake for 5 minutes at 400°F, then 15 minutes at 325°F. Cool on a wire rack. Repeat to cook all the pastries.

9 Place the slivered almonds in a single layer in a heatproof dish. Toast for 4–6 minutes at 325°F. Check and stir often, as they can burn quickly.

10 Heat the apricot jam in a small saucepan over low heat for 2–3 minutes, then brush over the pastries. Place the toasted almonds around the edge.

11 Dust with powdered sugar and serve fresh.

KEEP IT Make ahead to the end of step 5, cover, and leave in the fridge overnight. Or freeze for 6 weeks, separated by parchment paper. Defrost for 20 minutes before baking.

Prep + cook time
45 minutes
Makes 6

STRAWBERRY & YOGURT SHORTCAKES

4 tbsp (50ml) milk, plus extra
   for brushing
juice of ½ lemon
1 cup plus 2 tbsp (150g) all-purpose
   flour, plus extra for dusting
3 tbsp (40g) sugar, plus 1 tbsp
   for topping
¾ tsp baking powder
4 tbsp (60g) cold butter
1 egg, beaten

TOPPING:
8oz (225g) strawberries, hulled
   and sliced
1 tbsp honey, plus extra to serve
juice of ½ lemon
¾ cup (160g) Greek yogurt
1 tsp vanilla extract

1 Start by combining the milk with the lemon juice, and set aside. Combine the flour, sugar, and baking powder in a bowl, then grate the cold butter into the bowl, using the largest side on a box grater.

2 Pour the milk and lemon mixture into the bowl along with the beaten egg.

3 Using your hand in a claw shape, combine the mixture into a rough dough until everything is combined but there are still visible pieces of butter.

4 Pour the dough out onto a lightly floured surface. Bring it together into a rectangle about 1in (2.5cm) thick.

5 Roll the dough into a 8 x 4in (20 x 10cm) rectangle. Fold it in half, rotate it 90°, then roll out again to a 8 x 4in (20 x 10cm) rectangle. Fold in half again and pat with your hands to seal the top layer to the bottom layer.

6 Cut the dough in half to make two rectangular shortcakes. Brush with milk and sprinkle with sugar.

7 Preheat the air fryer to 350°F for 3 minutes.

8 Place the shortcakes directly into the basket and bake for 16 minutes.

9 For the topping, combine the strawberries with the honey and lemon juice in a bowl, and set aside. Combine the Greek yogurt and vanilla in a mixing bowl, and whisk for 2 minutes.

10 Let the shortcakes cool for 5–10 minutes.

11 To serve, cut open the shortcakes, top with generous dollops of yogurt, some macerated strawberries, and an extra drizzle of honey.

Prep + cook time
30 minutes
Makes 2

SEEDED BREAKFAST BAGELS

1 tsp active dried yeast
⅔ cup (150ml) lukewarm water
1¾ cups (250g) bread flour, plus
    extra for dusting
1 tbsp sugar
½ tsp sea salt
1 tsp baking soda
2 tbsp sesame, nigella, poppy,
    or sunflower seeds
flaked sea salt
vegetable oil cooking spray

FILLING SUGGESTIONS:
smoked salmon, cream cheese,
    pickles, and leafy greens
peanut butter and jelly
fried egg, hash brown, and sausage

1 Sprinkle the yeast over the warm water and stir to combine. Set aside for a couple of minutes until the yeast begins to foam. Spray five small squares of parchment paper with cooking oil spray. Set aside.

2 Place the flour, sugar, and salt in a large bowl. Stir briefly, so the sugar and salt are distributed, then add the yeasted water. Bring it together with a wooden spoon until you have a shaggy dough.

3 Pour the dough out onto a floured surface and knead for 5–8 minutes until you have a smooth, bouncy dough. Alternatively, use a stand mixer with a dough hook attachment.

4 Divide the dough into five pieces, and roll each piece into a ball. Using your hand like a claw, roll it in circular motions, pressing gently with your palm. Press a hole into the center of each ball with your index finger; twirl it around your finger to create the bagel shape.

5 Place each bagel on an oiled square of parchment paper on a baking sheet, spray lightly with oil, and cover with plastic wrap. Let rise in a warm place for 30 minutes–1 hour, or until doubled in size.

6 Bring a large pan of water to a boil and add the baking soda. Add one bagel at a time into the boiling water (use the paper to add them in). Boil for 30 seconds on each side. Drain on a wire rack.

7 Preheat the air fryer to 350°F for 3 minutes.

8 Spray the bagels with oil, then sprinkle with seeds and flaked sea salt. Place in the air fryer basket and bake for 12 minutes at 350°F until golden.

9 Transfer to a wire rack and cool for 10 minutes.

KEEP IT Store in an airtight container for up to 5 days.

Prep + cook time
1 hour 30 minutes
Makes 5

CHEESY BEAN PASTRIES

1 x 11oz (320g) sheet of puff pastry
½ cup (50g) grated mozzarella cheese
½ cup (50g) grated Cheddar cheese
1 egg, beaten

BAKED BEANS:
1 shallot, finely diced
2 tbsp olive oil
1 x 15.5oz (439g) can white beans, drained
1 x 14.5oz (411g) can diced tomatoes
½ tsp smoked paprika
½ tsp garlic powder
1 tbsp nutritional yeast
1 tbsp light brown sugar
½ tsp salt
black pepper, to taste
to serve: ketchup (optional)

TIP You will have a portion of beans left. Enjoy them with your favorite burger or hot dog.

1 Preheat the air fryer to 350°F for 3 minutes.

2 For the beans, put the diced shallot inside a 4-cup (1-liter) silicone liner or heatproof dish, drizzle with the olive oil, and season. Stir to coat, then roast for 8 minutes at 350°F.

3 Add the remaining baked beans ingredients and 3½ tablespoons water, season with freshly ground black pepper, and combine. Bake at 350°F for 20 minutes, stir, then bake for a further 30 minutes.

4 Spread the baked beans onto a baking sheet to help them cool quickly.

5 Unroll the pastry and cut vertically into three strips. Place two generous spoons of cooled beans on the top half of each strip, leaving a ¾in (2cm) gap around the sides. Top with one-quarter of the cheeses.

6 Brush the edges of the pastry with beaten egg, then fold the bottom half over, pushing down gently to seal the pastry.

7 Trim the edges, then use a fork to crimp the sealed sides. Brush with egg, then cut a ¾in (2cm) slit in the center of the pastry (for steam to escape). Sprinkle with the remaining cheese.

8 Place in the fridge for 20 minutes to firm up.

9 Preheat the air fryer to 400°F for 3 minutes.

10 Place them directly into the basket and bake for 10 minutes at 400°F, then for 15 minutes at 325°F. Let cool slightly before serving.

KEEP IT Make to the end of step 7, cover, and keep in the fridge overnight. Or freeze for 6 weeks, separated by parchment paper. Defrost for 30 minutes prior to baking.

**Prep + cook time
1 hour 30 minutes,
plus chilling
Makes 3**

SHAKSHUKA PASTRY CUPS

1 tbsp finely chopped cilantro stalks
1 garlic clove, finely chopped
½ tsp smoked paprika
1 tsp ground cumin
1 tsp chili flakes
½ tsp salt
black pepper, to taste
1 tbsp olive oil, plus extra
    for drizzling
1 x 14.5oz (411g) can diced tomatoes
½ x 11oz (320g) sheet of puff pastry
4 eggs
to serve: Greek yogurt and
    cilantro leaves

1 Preheat the air fryer to 350°F for 3 minutes.
2 Start by making the spiced tomato sauce. Add the cilantro stalks, garlic, spices, salt, a few grinds of black pepper, and the oil to a heatproof dish or silicone tray. Roast at 350°F for 3 minutes.
3 Pour in the chopped tomatoes, combine, and roast for a further 15 minutes. Remove from the air fryer and set aside to cool.
4 Cut four 4in (10cm) squares of pastry. Place each piece of pastry into a small ramekin, using your thumbs to push the pastry up the sides to create a cup.
5 Fill each cup with a tablespoon of the cooled tomato sauce.
6 Crack an egg into each cup, then top gently with another tablespoon of sauce. Season and drizzle with olive oil.
7 Preheat the air fryer to 350°F for 3 minutes.
8 Bake the shakshuka cups for 16 minutes at 350°F for a runny yolk center, or 20 minutes for a hard yolk.
9 Let cool for 5 minutes before removing from the ramekins, then serve warm with a dollop of Greek yogurt and a few cilantro leaves.

Prep + cook time
30 minutes
Makes 4

FRITTATA MUFFINS (GLUTEN-FREE)

6 eggs
⅓ cup (100ml) milk
2 tbsp snipped chives
½ tsp garlic powder
1 tsp salt
black pepper, to taste
to serve: ketchup (optional)

SUPER GREENS AND FETA FILLING:
1/2 cup (30g) of spinach
1 small bunch of dill, thick stalks
    removed
1 small bunch of cilantro, thick
    stalks removed
3½oz (100g) feta, crumbled
black pepper, to taste

ROASTED VEGGIE FILLING:
1 green bell pepper, diced
1 zucchini, diced
⅓ cup (50g) frozen corn
1 tsp olive oil
½ tsp chili flakes
½ tsp salt

BACON AND CHEDDAR FILLING:
7oz (200g) chopped bacon
1 cup (100g) grated Cheddar cheese
black pepper, to taste

1 Make your choice of filling. For the super greens and feta filling, roughly chop the spinach and herbs. Add to a small food processor or blender with 1 tablespoon water, and blend until it resembles a chunky pesto. Stir in the crumbled feta, and season with black pepper.

2 For the roasted veggie filling, preheat the air fryer to 400°F for 3 minutes. Combine the ingredients in a heatproof dish, and roast for 20 minutes at 400°F until charred.

3 For the bacon and cheddar filling, preheat the air fryer to 400°F for 3 minutes. Place the bacon directly into the air fryer, and cook at 400°F for 8 minutes, or until crispy. Let cool on a paper towel, then combine with the grated cheese and some black pepper.

4 To make the frittata, combine the eggs, milk, chives, garlic powder, salt, and plenty of black pepper in a large bowl. Whisk until silky, then pour the mixture into a measuring cup with a spout.

5 Preheat the air fryer to 350°F for 3 minutes.

6 Place 12 silicone muffin cases directly into the air fryer basket (or cook in batches), then fill each case three-quarters full with your chosen filling. Fill each case with the egg, leaving ¼in (5mm) space for the muffins to rise.

7 Bake for 12 minutes at 350°F; if they're still very wobbly, bake for a further 3 minutes.

8 Let cool in the cases for 5 minutes before removing.

KEEP IT Store for up to 3 days in an airtight container in the fridge.

Prep + cook time
30 minutes
Makes 12

SNACKS

When you are in need of a little pick-me-up, the air fryer is your friend. The hot circulating air creates the crispiest pastry twists and seedy bagel straws. For a more substantial snack to please a crowd, try Mini Pizzas 3 Ways (see p44) or Kimchi & Grilled Cheese (see p43).

EVERYTHING BAGEL STRAWS

1 x 11oz (320g) sheet of puff pastry
1 egg, beaten

EVERYTHING BAGEL MIX:
2 tbsp white sesame seeds
1 tbsp black sesame seeds
1 tbsp poppy seeds
½ tsp garlic powder
½ tsp onion powder
1 tsp salt
1 tsp coarse black pepper

SOUR CREAM DIP:
⅔ cup (150g) sour cream
¼ cup (25g) pickles of your choice,
    finely diced (onion, gherkin,
    capers, etc.)
1 tsp spicy mustard
1 tbsp snipped chives

1 Combine all the everything bagel mix ingredients in a small bowl, then set aside.

2 Unroll the pastry sheet, keeping it on the paper, and brush with the beaten egg. Sprinkle the whole sheet in the seed mix; you want the whole surface to be covered, but you may not need it all.

3 Cut the pastry in half crosswise, then cut both pieces into 1in (2.5cm) thick strips.

4 Preheat the air fryer to 350°F for 3 minutes.

5 Working in batches, place the strips directly into the air fryer basket, seeded-side up, leaving a ¾in (2cm) gap between each strip, as they will double in size. Bake at 350°F for 10 minutes.

6 While the pastry is baking, combine the dip ingredients and season to taste.

7 Serve the straws with the dip. They are best served fresh but can be reheated just before serving, if necessary.

TIP You can save any remaining seed mix to top soups, salads, or eggs.

Prep + cook time
30 minutes
Makes 32

PADRÓN PEPPER POPPERS

8 fresh padrón or shishito peppers
1⅓ cups (300g) cream cheese, softened
1 egg, beaten
4 tbsp (30g) all-purpose flour
1 tsp garlic powder
salt and black pepper, to taste
1½ cups (60g) panko bread crumbs
¾ cup (50g) finely grated Parmesan cheese
vegetable or olive oil cooking spray

1 Prepare the peppers. Wash and dry them, then slice off the tops and carefully remove the inner stems.
2 Fill a piping bag with the cream cheese (or use a sandwich bag and snip the corner off). Fill each pepper with cream cheese, then set aside while you prepare the coating.
3 Place the egg in a wide-based bowl. Mix the flour with the garlic powder in another bowl and season with salt and pepper. Put the bread crumbs and Parmesan cheese in a third bowl.
4 Working in batches, dust the stuffed peppers lightly in flour, then coat in the egg, then roll in the bread crumb and cheese mixture.

5 Preheat the air fryer to 350°F for 3 minutes.
6 Place the peppers directly into the preheated air fryer basket, spray with oil, and bake at 350°F for 12 minutes.
7 Serve immediately.

SERVE IT Serve hot with a bowl of sweet chili sauce for dipping or a drizzle of hot honey and plenty of flaked sea salt.

**Prep + cook time
30 minutes
Makes 16**

CHEDDAR SCONES

2 cups (250g) all-purpose flour, plus
  extra for dusting
1 tsp baking powder
5 tbsp (70g) butter, cold
2 cups (200g) grated Cheddar
  cheese
⅓ cup (100ml) milk, plus extra for
  brushing
1 tsp spicy mustard
1 tsp sea salt
1 tsp ground black pepper

1 Place the flour and baking powder in a medium mixing bowl, then grate in the cold butter using the largest side of a box grater.

2 Rub the butter into the flour using your fingertips until the mix resembles fine bread crumbs. Stir in 1½ cups (150g) of the Cheddar cheese.

3 Whisk the milk, mustard, salt, and pepper together, then pour into the flour mix. Using a spoon, combine until it resembles a shaggy dough. Pour out the dough onto a lightly floured work surface.

4 Knead gently until the dough just comes together, then shape into a circle about 2in (5cm) thick. Cut it into six triangles. Place on a parchment paper–lined baking sheet, cover, and chill for at least 30 minutes (or up to overnight).

5 Preheat the air fryer to 400°F for 3 minutes.

6 Brush each scone with milk, then sprinkle with the remaining cheese.

7 Place directly into the air fryer basket and bake for 15 minutes at 400°F. Let cool before serving.

SERVE IT Cut them open and serve with salted butter, ham, mustard, and pickles.

**Prep + cook time
45 minutes, plus chilling
Makes 6**

MINI SAVORY GALETTES

3 cups (400g) whole wheat flour, plus extra for dusting
1 tbsp nigella seeds
1 tsp salt
½ cup plus 5 tbsp (200g) cold butter
2 tbsp cold water
1lb (450g) seasonal veggies, such as asparagus
drizzle of olive oil
¼ cup chopped herbs, such as parsley, basil, tarragon, or chives
salt and black pepper, to taste
1 egg, beaten
to serve: pickled red onion

FILLING:
1 cup (250g) ricotta
1 egg
½ cup (40g) finely grated Parmesan cheese, plus extra to serve
1 garlic clove

1 Place the flour in a large mixing bowl and combine with the nigella seeds and salt. Grate the cold butter into the bowl, using the largest side on a box grater. Add the cold water.

2 Using your fingertips, rub the butter into the flour. As the dough starts to clump, use your hand to bring it into a ball. Don't worry if there are still flecks of butter, you just want all the flour absorbed. Wrap in plastic wrap and put in the fridge for 20 minutes.

3 Meanwhile, combine the filling ingredients in a bowl.

4 Prepare the veggies as needed. If using any root vegetables, be sure to slice thinly or part-roast. Toss in olive oil, the herbs, and some salt and pepper.

5 Cut the chilled dough into eight equal pieces and roll into rough balls.

6 On a floured surface, roll out into 6in (15cm) circles.

7 Divide the ricotta filling among the pastry circles.

Spread the mixture out, but leave a 1¼in (3cm) border.

8 Layer the veggies on top, then fold in the edges of the pastry, pushing the corners to seal in the toppings. Brush the edges with egg. If the pastry has softened, transfer to a lined baking sheet and chill for 30 minutes.

9 Preheat the air fryer to 350°F for 3 minutes.

10 Using a spatula, place the galettes directly into the basket. Bake at 350°F for 20 minutes until the pastry is golden and the base is crisp.

11 Cool for 5–10 minutes before serving topped with Parmesan cheese and some pickled red onion.

KEEP IT Keep for 3 days in an airtight container in the fridge. Reheat in the air fryer.

Prep + cook time
1 hour, plus chilling
Makes 8

KIMCHI GRILLED CHEESE

2 tbsp (30g) salted butter, softened
4 large slices of bread
2 tsp hot sauce, plus extra to serve
2 tbsp kimchi
1 green onion
2oz (60g) mozzarella cheese, sliced
2 tbsp sesame seeds

1 Butter each side of the bread. Trim off the crusts.
2 Spread 1 teaspoon hot sauce on two slices of the bread, then place 1 tablespoon kimchi in the center of the slice, along with half of the mozzarella, making sure to leave a ¾in (2cm) border around the edge of the slice.
3 Place a buttered piece of bread on top, and, using the sides of your hands, push down the border to seal the filling inside.
4 Place the sesame seeds on a plate, then push each side of the buttered sandwiches into the seeds until they are evenly coated. Cut a ½in (1cm) hole in the center of the bread for the steam to escape as they bake.

5 Preheat the air fryer to 350°F for 3 minutes.
6 Place the sandwiches directly into the air fryer basket and bake for 8 minutes at 350°F. Flip the toast over, then bake for a further 3 minutes.
7 Let cool for 5 minutes before cutting in half and serving with extra hot sauce.

**Prep + cook time
30 minutes
Makes 2**

MINI PIZZAS 3 WAYS

1½ cups (200g) all-purpose flour, plus extra for dusting
1 cup (200g) plain yogurt
1½ tsp baking powder
1 tsp salt

TOPPINGS
3½oz (100g) basil and oregano pizza sauce or fresh basil pesto
4oz (125g) ball of mozzarella cheese, torn
4oz (125g) toppings of your choice
salt and black pepper, to taste

TIP For a tomato base: try adding chopped bacon, or alternatively go for marinated red peppers or sun-dried tomatoes, and finish with some basil leaves once cooked.

For a basil pesto base: try topping with thinly sliced zucchini, chili flakes, and lemon zest, and finishing with shaved Parmesan cheese once cooked.

1 Combine the flour, yogurt, baking powder, and salt in a bowl, and mix with a wooden spoon until fully combined. Once it starts to form a soft ball of dough, use your hand to bring it together. If it is still sticky, sprinkle in a little extra flour until you can handle the dough easily.

2 Scrape the dough out onto a lightly floured surface, and knead for 2 minutes to bring it together into a smooth ball. This isn't like a regular yeasted pizza dough, so it doesn't require lots of kneading. Place a clean kitchen towel over the dough.

3 Get all of your pizza toppings ready.

4 Preheat the air fryer to 400°F for 3 minutes.

5 Cut the dough into six pieces. On the floured work surface, use your hands to gently push out the dough into 4in (10cm) circles.

6 Dust off any excess flour, then top your pizzas with your chosen toppings and season with salt and black pepper. Gently transfer to the preheated air fryer using a flour-dusted spatula to place the pizzas directly onto the rack (the pizzas will increase in size, so be sure to leave a 1in/ 2.5cm gap between them).

7 Cook at 400°F for 8–12 minutes, or until the base is crisp. Serve hot.

KEEP IT They will keep for 3 days in the fridge. Use the reheat setting on the air fryer to warm them through, or serve cold.

**Prep + cook time
30 minutes
Makes 6**

ONE-BOWL YOGURT CAKES

1 cup (200g) plain yogurt
½ cup (120ml) vegetable oil
2 eggs
¾ cup (150g) sugar
1 tsp vanilla extract
grated zest of ½ lemon
1⅓ cups (180g) all-purpose flour
1¼ tsp baking powder
½ tsp salt

1 Combine the yogurt, oil, eggs, sugar, vanilla, and lemon zest in a large mixing bowl, then sift in the flour, baking powder, and salt. Combine with a whisk until you have a smooth batter.

2 Place 12 silicone cupcake cases (lined with paper cases, if you like) into the air fryer basket. Using a cookie scoop or spoon, fill the cases three-quarters full.

3 Preheat the air fryer to 325°F for 3 minutes.

4 Bake at 325°F for 15 minutes.

5 Remove the basket from the air fryer and let cool for 5 minutes before lifting the cakes out.

6 Remove the cakes from the silicone cases when still slightly warm, then let cool fully on a wire rack.

TIP Store in an airtight container for up to 5 days.

**Prep + cook time
30 minutes
Makes 12**

JAM TWISTS WITH RASPBERRY JAM DIP

1 x 11oz (320g) sheet of puff pastry
½ cup (50g) slivered almonds
1 cup (150g) powdered sugar
5 raspberries
juice of 1 lemon

FRANGIPANE:
4 tbsp (60g) salted butter, softened
¼ cup (50g) sugar
1 egg
¾ cup (80g) ground almonds
1 tbsp milk, plus extra for brushing
1 tsp almond extract
3 tbsp (25g) all-purpose flour

RASPBERRY JAM DIP:
5oz (140g) frozen or fresh
   raspberries
5 tbsp (60g) sugar
grated zest of 1 lemon

1 For the frangipane, beat the butter and sugar with a wooden spoon for 2–3 minutes. Add the egg, almonds, milk, and almond extract, and combine. Fold in the flour. Set aside.

2 Unroll the pastry sheet, keeping it on the paper. Using the back of a spoon, spread the frangipane across the pastry. Use the paper to help you fold the pastry in half lengthwise. Wrap it in its paper and place on a baking sheet. Chill for 20 minutes.

3 Preheat the air fryer to 350°F for 3 minutes.

4 Place the slivered almonds in a single layer in a heatproof dish. Toast for 2 minutes at 350°F. Stir, then bake for a further 2 minutes, or until golden brown. Set aside.

5 To make the jam dip, crush the raspberries in a bowl with the sugar and lemon zest, then transfer to a heatproof dish.

6 Cook for 10 minutes at 350°F. Stir, then cook for 5 minutes more. Set aside to cool.

7 Cut the chilled pastry crosswise into 1in (2.5cm) thick strips. Twist each strip, then brush with milk.

8 Put the twists into the air fryer basket (in batches), leaving a ¾in (2cm) gap between them. Bake at 350°F for 12 minutes.

9 Sift the powdered sugar into a large bowl. In a small bowl, crush the 5 raspberries with the back of a fork, and combine with the lemon juice. Add to the powdered sugar, and mix well.

10 Place the twists on a wire rack. Brush with the raspberry glaze while still warm, then sprinkle with the almonds before it sets. Serve with the dip! Best eaten on the same day.

**Prep + cook time
45 minutes, plus chilling
Makes 12**

TROPICAL FRUIT & COCONUT BARS
(GLUTEN-FREE)

1 cup (220g) butter
3 tbsp (60g) honey
½ cup (100g) light brown sugar
2 cups (200g) old-fashioned oats
1 cup (80g) dried flaked coconut
1½ tbsp (10g) poppy or chia seeds
3oz (80g) dried mango, chopped into small chunks
2oz (50g) dried pineapple, chopped into small chunks
1½ tsp salt

1 Preheat the air fryer to 350°F for 3 minutes.
2 Combine the butter, honey, and sugar in a heatproof dish. Place in the air fryer for 4 minutes at 350°F. The mixture should be melted and starting to bubble.
3 Combine all the remaining dry ingredients in a large mixing bowl. Pour in the hot syrup, and stir with a spoon until all the oats are coated.
4 Pour the mixture into a 8in (20cm) parchment paper–lined brownie pan, then press down with the back of the spoon; the mix should be compact and even.

5 Place the pan into the air fryer basket and bake for 16 minutes at 350°F.
6 Let cool in the pan on a wire rack. Once cooled, turn out of the pan and cut into eight rectangles.

KEEP IT Will keep for up to 7 days in an airtight container.

Prep + cook time
30 minutes
Makes 8

PASTEL DE NATA

1 x 11oz (320g) sheet of puff pastry
1 tsp ground cinnamon,
    plus extra to decorate
all-purpose flour, for dusting
1 cup (250ml) vanilla custard

1 Unroll the puff pastry sheet, keeping it on the paper. Sprinkle the whole piece of pastry with ground cinnamon.
2 Taking one of the long edges, roll the pastry into a tight swirl.
3 Cut the pastry into eight pieces. On a lightly floured work surface, roll each piece of pastry into a 3–4in (7.5–10cm) circle.
4 Preheat the air fryer to 400°F for 3 minutes.
5 Place each circle of pastry into a small ramekin, gently pushing the pastry into it.

6 Fill each pastry case two-thirds full with custard, then place into the air fryer basket, and bake for 16 minutes at 400°F.
7 Let cool in the ramekins for 10 minutes before removing and serving warm with a dusting of cinnamon.

**Prep + cook time
30 minutes
Makes 8**

COOKIES & BROWNIES

The ease of the air fryer will take you by surprise when it comes to baking cookies—simply line the basket with a silicone mat or parchment paper, and cook them in batches. As for brownies and blondies, just make sure that your pan fits in your air fryer and you're good to go!

BIRTHDAY CAKE SANDWICH COOKIES

¾ cup (200g) butter, softened
6 tbsp (50g) powdered sugar
1½ cups (200g) all-purpose flour
6½ tbsp (40g) cornstarch
1 tsp vanilla extract
1 tsp salt
⅔ cup (100g) white chocolate chips
3 tbsp sprinkles, plus extra
  to decorate

BUTTERCREAM FILLING:
7 tbsp (100g) butter, softened
1½ cups (200g) powdered sugar,
  sifted
½ cup (100g) cream cheese
1 tsp vanilla extract
1 tsp salt

1 Combine the butter and powdered sugar in a mixing bowl, and beat with a wooden spoon for 2 minutes. Add the flour, cornstarch, vanilla, and salt, and mix until a soft dough forms. Fold in the chocolate chips and sprinkles. Cover the dough and chill for a minimum of 1 hour (and up to 1 day).

2 Prepare the buttercream filling while your dough is chilling. Place the softened butter in a large mixing bowl, and gradually add the sifted powdered sugar, beating until fluffy. If you have an electric hand mixer, use this to speed up the process. Add the cream cheese, vanilla, and salt, then beat until combined. Set aside in the fridge.

3 Using a tablespoon measuring spoon, portion the dough into 24 scoops. Roll them into balls.

4 Preheat the air fryer to 325°F for 3 minutes. Line with parchment paper.

5 Working in batches, if necessary, place the dough balls into the preheated lined air fryer basket, leaving a 2in (5cm) gap between them, as they will expand. Bake at 325°F for 12 minutes.

6 Let the cookies cool for 5 minutes before removing them from the air fryer basket with a spatula. Place on a wire rack to cool completely. Repeat the process until all the cookies are baked.

7 Take two cookies and sandwich them together with a spoonful of the buttercream filling, squeezing them together until the filling just escapes the sides. Roll the sides of each sandwiched cookie in sprinkles to decorate.

KEEP IT These will keep for 3 days in an airtight container in the fridge.

**Prep + cook time
1 hour, plus chilling
Makes 12**

DOUBLE-DECKER BROWNIE COOKIE SQUARES

COOKIE DOUGH:

5½ tbsp (80g) butter, softened

7 tbsp (80g) light brown sugar

1 egg, beaten

1 tsp vanilla extract

1 cup (120g) all-purpose flour

½ tsp baking powder

½ tsp baking soda

1 tsp sea salt

1 cup (150g) milk chocolate chips

BROWNIE BATTER:

3½oz (100g) dark chocolate, roughly
  chopped

4 tbsp (60g) butter, cubed

7 tbsp (80g) light brown sugar

1 egg, beaten

½ tsp salt

2 tbsp (20g) all-purpose flour, sifted

1 cup (150g) white chocolate chips

1 For the cookie dough, beat the butter and sugar with a wooden spoon, then mix in the egg and vanilla. Sift in the flour, backing powder, baking soda, and salt. Mix until smooth, then fold in the chocolate chips.

2 Scrape the dough into an 8in (20cm) lined brownie pan, pressing it in evenly. Place in the fridge and then make the brownie batter.

3 Melt the chocolate and butter in a small heatproof bowl set over a pan of simmering water, stirring. Remove from the heat and check the temperature of the mixture: it should be warm, not hot (if it's hot, let it cool for 5 minutes).

4 Whisk the sugar and egg together in a mixing bowl, then pour in the warm chocolate-butter mixture. Whisk until combined. Add the salt and flour, then fold in with a spatula. Fold in the chocolate chips.

5 Preheat the air fryer to 350°F for 3 minutes, and remove the pan from the fridge.

6 Bake in the air fryer for 10 minutes at 180°C/ 350°F. Tap on the surface to deflate the dough, then pour over the brownie batter, and smooth it with a spatula. Bake at 180°C/ 350°F for 14 minutes until it has a crisp crust, but a slight wobble. Cool in the tin on a wire rack, then put in the fridge to chill for 2–3 hours.

7 Once set, remove from the tin and cut into squares.

KEEP IT Keep for up to 5 days in an airtight container in the fridge.

**Prep + cook time
40 minutes, plus chilling
Makes 12**

OATMEAL, CANDIED ORANGE & RAISIN COOKIES

7 tbsp (100g) butter, softened
¾ cup (150g) light brown sugar
1 egg
1 cup (100g) old-fashioned oats
1½ cups (200g) all-purpose flour
½ tsp baking soda
½ tsp baking powder
1 tsp ground cinnamon
1 tsp salt
⅓ cup (45g) candied orange peel
½ cup (75g) raisins

1 Combine the softened butter and brown sugar in a large mixing bowl, and beat for 2 minutes until the mixture starts to become lighter in texture. Add the egg and oats, and mix until fully incorporated.

2 Sift in the flour, baking soda, baking powder, cinnamon, and salt, and fold these into the batter until you have a soft cookie dough consistency. Finally, fold in the orange peel and raisins until evenly distributed.

3 Using a scale, weigh out 1¾oz (50g) portions of dough. Roll each one between the palms of your hands and place in a parchment paper–lined airtight container (if you are double layering, separate the layers of cookie dough with a piece of parchment paper) and place in the fridge for at least 1 hour or overnight.

4 Preheat the air fryer to 340°F for 3 minutes and line the basket with a silicone mat or parchment paper.

5 Put the chilled cookie dough portions into the lined preheated air fryer basket, leaving 2in (5cm) between each cookie. Bake for 15 minutes at 340°F.

6 Let the cookies cool for 5 minutes before removing them from the air fryer basket with a spatula. Place on a wire rack to cool completely.

KEEP IT Store for up to 5 days in an airtight container.

**Prep + cook time
30 minutes, plus chilling
Makes 12**

BROWN BUTTER & SALTED PECAN BLONDIES

¾ cup (200g) butter, cubed
1½ cups (300g) light brown sugar
2 eggs
2 tsp vanilla extract
2 cups (250g) all-purpose flour
2 tsp cornstarch
⅔ cup (100g) white chocolate chips
¾ cup (75g) pecan halves, roughly chopped
2 tsp flaked sea salt

1 Place the butter in a small saucepan over low heat. The butter will start to bubble and foam, then caramelize, and small brown flecks will start to appear. This will take 10–15 minutes, but keep checking and swirling the pan every couple of minutes, as it can suddenly change from golden to burnt. Once the liquid has turned a deep golden brown and smells toasted, remove from the heat and transfer the hot butter into a heatproof bowl to cool for 15 minutes.

2 Combine the cooled brown butter, sugar, eggs, and vanilla in a large mixing bowl, and whisk until the sugar has dissolved. Sift in the flour and cornstarch, and mix until just combined, then add the chocolate chips and pecans. Give the batter a good mix until everything is evenly distributed.

3 Preheat the air fryer to 325°F for 3 minutes.
4 Pour the blondie batter into an 8in (20cm) parchment paper–lined brownie pan, and sprinkle with the flaked sea salt. Bake in the preheated air fryer at 325°F for 35 minutes until evenly golden with a firm crust, but a soft center.
5 Let cool in the pan on a wire rack for 30 minutes, then place in the fridge to set overnight (or for at least 3 hours) before cutting into 9 large or 20 bite-sized pieces.

KEEP IT These will last for 5 days in an airtight container in the fridge, or can be frozen for up to 6 weeks.

Prep + cook time
1 hour, plus chilling
Makes 9 large or 20 bites

CHOCOLATE & HAZELNUT THUMBPRINT COOKIES

6 tbsp (75g) butter, softened

4½ tbsp (40g) powdered sugar

1 tsp vanilla extract

1 egg yolk

1 cup (125g) all-purpose flour, plus extra for dusting

1 cup (150g) hazelnuts, chopped

2 tsp flaked sea salt

½ cup (150g) chocolate hazelnut spread

1 Beat the butter, powdered sugar, vanilla, and egg yolk in a mixing bowl with a wooden spoon until combined. Mix in the flour until a soft dough forms.

2 Lay a 16in/40cm piece of plastic wrap on the work surface. Place the dough in the center, and, using your hands, squeeze the dough to form a chunky sausage about 12in (30cm) long. Wrap it in the plastic wrap, and place in the fridge for 20 minutes.

3 Place the chilled dough on a lightly floured surface. Slice the log into 10 pieces, roughly 1¼in (3cm) thick. Using your palms, roll each piece into a ball.

4 Combine the chopped hazelnuts and flaked sea salt in a shallow bowl. One by one, place each dough ball into the mix, and roll it to coat in a layer of nuts.

5 Using a tablespoon measuring spoon, make an indent in the center of each cookie.

6 Preheat the air fryer to 325°F for 3 minutes and line the basket with a silicone mat or parchment paper.

7 Put the cookies in the lined preheated air fryer basket, leaving 2in (5cm) between each cookie. You may need to bake them in batches.

8 Bake at 325°F for 10–12 minutes until lightly golden brown. Continue to bake in batches until all the cookies are cooked.

9 Press down in the center with the tablespoon measuring spoon again while they are still hot (as they will have puffed up slightly while cooking).

10 While still warm, spoon the chocolate hazelnut spread into the indents, and let cool.

KEEP IT These will keep for 5 days in an airtight container.

**Prep + cook time
40 minutes, plus chilling
Makes 10**

SESAME & DARK CHOCOLATE COOKIES

9 tbsp (125g) butter

⅓ cup (30g) unsweetened cocoa powder

1 egg, beaten

⅓ cup (80g) light brown sugar

⅓ cup (80g) sugar

1 cup plus 1 tbsp (140g) all-purpose flour

½ tsp baking soda

1 cup (150g) dark chocolate chips

5 tbsp sesame seeds

1 tsp sea salt (optional)

1 Place the butter in a small saucepan on a low heat until melted, then stir in the cocoa until it becomes smooth and lump-free. Remove from heat and set aside.

2 In a large mixing bowl, combine the egg with the sugars, and whisk until the sugars have dissolved. Pour in the lukewarm melted butter and cocoa mix. Whisk again until combined.

3 Sift the flour and baking soda into the batter, then stir until a soft dough forms. Once all the flour is absorbed, fold in the chocolate chips. Place the dough in the fridge for 30 minutes to firm up.

4 Once the dough has chilled, weigh out 2oz (60g) portions and roll into balls using the palms of your hands. Spread the sesame seeds out in a shallow bowl, then roll each dough ball in the seeds to coat.

5 Place the coated dough balls back into the fridge for 30 minutes (or up to overnight).

6 Preheat the air fryer to 350°F for 3 minutes and line the basket with a silicone mat or parchment paper.

7 Put the chilled cookie dough portions in the lined preheated air fryer basket, leaving 2in (5cm) between each cookie, sprinkle with sea salt, if using, and bake at 350°F for 10 minutes.

8 Let the cookies cool in the air fryer basket until firm enough to remove with a spatula, then transfer to a wire rack to cool completely.

KEEP IT These will keep for up to 5 days in an airtight container.

Prep + cook time
30 minutes, plus chilling
Makes 10

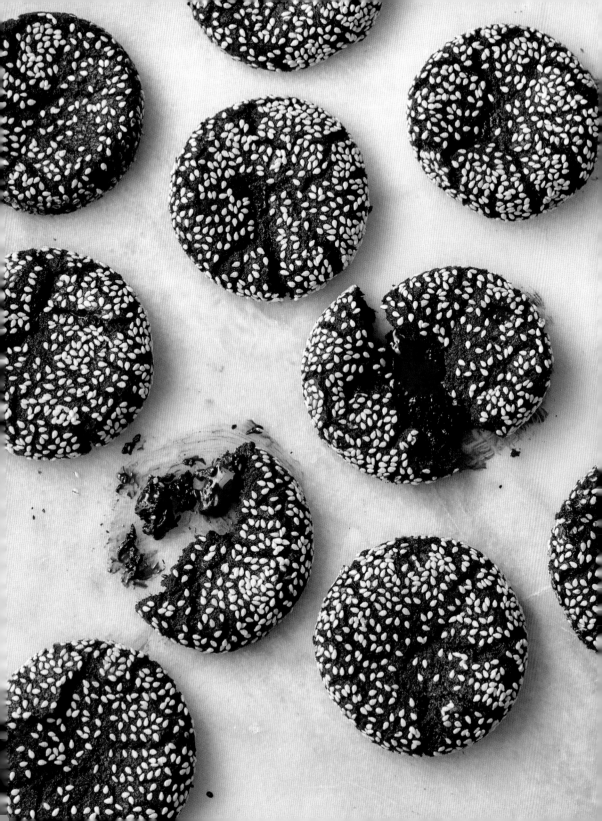

RASPBERRY CHEESECAKE BROWNIES

7oz (200g) dark chocolate, roughly chopped
½ cup (120g) butter, cubed
½ cup plus 4 tsp (120g) light brown sugar
2 eggs
¼ cup (35g) all-purpose flour
1 tsp salt
3½oz (100g) raspberries

CHEESECAKE:
⅔ cup (150g) cream cheese
1 egg
1 tsp vanilla extract
2 tbsp sugar
2 tsp cornstarch

1 Place the chocolate and butter in a heatproof bowl over a pan of simmering water. You want the bowl to rest 1in (2.5cm) above the water. Keep stirring until the chocolate has melted, then remove the bowl from the pan (taking care as the bowl will be very hot) and set aside to cool slightly.
2 Combine all the cheesecake ingredients in a medium mixing bowl and set aside.
3 In another mixing bowl, combine the brown sugar and eggs, and whisk until the sugar starts to dissolve. Pour in the warm melted chocolate, whisk until fully combined, then fold in the flour and salt.
4 Pour the brownie mixture into a parchment paper–lined 8in (20cm) brownie pan, and spread it out evenly. Dollop the cheesecake mixture over the top. Using a skewer or knife, swirl the two batters together.

5 Sprinkle the raspberries all over, pushing some down so they are half-submerged by the batter.
6 Preheat the air fryer to 325°F for 3 minutes.
7 Place the brownie pan in the preheated air fryer, and bake for 25 minutes at 325°F until the cheesecake mix has started to brown and form a crust (the mix should be firm, but have a wobble if you gently shake the pan).
8 Let cool in the pan on a wire rack for 30 minutes before placing in the fridge to set overnight (or for at least 3 hours).
9 Cut into 9 large or 20 bite-sized pieces.

**Prep + cook time
50 minutes, plus chilling
Makes 9 large or 20 bites**

SALTED PRETZEL, FUDGE & PEANUT COOKIES

5½ tbsp (80g) butter, softened
½ cup (100g) dark brown sugar
3 tbsp crunchy peanut butter
1 egg, beaten
1¼ cup (150g) all-purpose flour
½ tsp baking powder
½ tsp baking soda
1 tsp sea salt
3½oz (100g) fudge or caramel candy pieces
1oz (30g) salted pretzels, broken into pieces
2 tbsp (30g) roasted peanuts

1 In a large mixing bowl, combine the butter, sugar, and peanut butter. Beat with a wooden spoon until the mixture lightens. Add the egg and mix until combined. Sift in the flour, baking powder, and baking soda, then sprinkle in the sea salt. Mix until the flour is absorbed.

2 Fold in the fudge pieces, pretzel pieces, and roasted peanuts until evenly distributed.

3 Weigh the dough out into 2oz (50g) portions, then roll into balls using the palms of your hands. Place the rolled cookie dough onto a parchment paper– lined baking sheet and put in the fridge for at least 30 minutes (or up to overnight) to firm up.

4 Preheat the air fryer to 350°F for 3 minutes and line the basket with a silicone mat or parchment paper.

5 Carefully transfer each cookie to the lined air fryer basket, leaving 2in (5cm) between them. Bake for 10–12 minutes at 350°F until they're lightly golden brown.

6 Let the cookies cool in the air fryer basket until firm enough to remove with a spatula, then transfer to a wire rack to cool completely.

KEEP IT Store for up to 5 days in an airtight container.

Prep + cook time
30 minutes, plus chilling
Makes 10

ICED VANILLA COOKIES

5½ tbsp (75g) butter, softened
2½ tbsp (30g) sugar
½ tsp salt
1 tsp vanilla extract
¾ cup (100g) all-purpose flour

ICING:
1½ cups (200g) royal icing sugar
2–5 drops of food coloring

TIP If you can't find royal icing sugar, make your own by combining 3 cups (400g) sifted powdered sugar and 2 egg whites, and beating into a thick, smooth icing that will drizzle but hold its form.

1 Beat the butter, sugar, salt, and vanilla in a mixing bowl with a wooden spoon until light and fluffy. Sift in the flour and stir until a soft dough forms.

2 Weigh the dough into ¾oz (20g) portions, then roll into balls with the palms of your hands. Place onto a parchment paper–lined baking sheet with a 2in (5cm) gap between them. Using a flat-bottomed glass, press each ball to flatten it. Chill in the fridge for 30 minutes.

3 Preheat the air fryer to 350°F for 3 minutes and line the basket with a silicone mat or parchment paper.

4 Transfer each cookie to the lined air fryer basket. Bake for 8–12 minutes at 350°F until they're lightly golden brown.

5 Leave in the basket for a few minutes, then transfer to a wire rack to cool.

6 For the icing, sift the royal icing sugar into a large mixing bowl, then add 2 tablespoons water, if needed.

7 Bring together with a spatula until you have a smooth icing, then whisk with a handheld electric mixer for 5 minutes until the mix doubles in size and leaves stiff peaks when you lift the beaters out of the bowl. At this point, you can color the icing—either divide among smaller bowls to make multiple colors or use just one (add the coloring drop by drop until you have your desired shade).

8 Put a piping bag fitted with a nozzle in a tall glass, rolling the excess over the sides. Spoon in the icing. Decorate the cookies in your chosen design, then let set for at least 1 hour (or up to overnight).

KEEP IT These will keep for 5–7 days in an airtight container.

Prep + cook time
30 minutes, plus chilling
Makes 10

CORNFLAKE COOKIES

7 tbsp (100g) butter, softened

½ cup (100g) light brown sugar

1 egg, beaten

1 tsp vanilla extract

1¼ cup (150g) all-purpose flour

½ tsp baking powder

½ tsp baking soda

1 tsp salt

2 cups (50g) cornflakes

5 tbsp (20g) freeze-dried strawberries

⅔ cup (100g) white chocolate chips

1 Combine the butter and sugar in a medium mixing bowl. Beat with a wooden spoon until combined, then pour in the egg and vanilla. Mix again until they start to come together (don't worry if the mixture looks split; as soon as you add the dry ingredients, a smooth dough will form).

2 Sift the flour, baking powder, baking soda, and salt into the bowl. Mix until all the flour is absorbed and you have a smooth cookie dough. Fold in the cornflakes, strawberries, and chocolate chips until they are evenly distributed.

3 Weigh the dough out into 2oz (50g) portions, then roll into balls using the palms of your hands. If the dough is very soft and sticky, place it in the fridge for 30 minutes to firm up before rolling into balls.

4 Place the rolled cookies on a parchment paper–lined baking sheet and put in the fridge for at least 30 minutes (or up to overnight) before baking.

5 Preheat the air fryer to 350°F for 3 minutes and line the basket with a silicone mat or parchment paper.

6 Put the cookies in the lined air fryer basket, leaving 2in (5cm) between each cookie. Bake for 10 minutes at 350°F, or until light golden brown.

7 Let cool in the air fryer basket until firm enough to remove with a spatula, then transfer to a wire rack to cool completely.

KEEP IT These cookies will keep for up to 5 days in an airtight container.

Prep + cook time
30 minutes, plus chilling
Makes 12

BROWNIE MUD PIE

10½oz (300g) dark chocolate,
    roughly chopped
¾ cup (180g) butter, cubed
1 cup (180g) light brown sugar
3 eggs, beaten
1 tsp sea salt
½ cup (60g) all-purpose flour
3½oz (100g) milk chocolate, chopped
100g (3½oz) dark chocolate,
    chopped

BASE:
7oz (200g) gingersnaps
5 tbsp (75g) butter, melted
1 tsp flaked sea salt

1 Start by making the base. Crush the gingersnaps into a fine sandy crumb in a food processor or by bashing with a rolling pin. Mix with the melted butter and sea salt.

2 Spoon the mixture into a greased 8–9in (20–23cm) loose-bottomed round pan. Use the back of a spoon to press the crumbs into the base and ½in (1cm) up the sides. Place in the fridge to chill while you make the brownie batter.

3 Melt the chocolate and butter in a small heatproof bowl set over a pan of simmering water, stirring. Remove from the heat and check the temperature of the mixture: it should be warm, not hot (if it's hot, let it cool for 5 minutes).

4 Whisk the sugar and eggs in a mixing bowl, then pour in the warm chocolate butter mix. Whisk until fully combined (the mixture should start to thicken as this happens).

5 Add the salt to the batter and sift in the flour, then fold these in with a spatula until the flour is all absorbed. Add the chopped chocolate and fold in until evenly distributed.

6 Preheat the air fryer to 325°F for 3 minutes.

7 Remove the pan from the fridge and pour in the brownie batter. Place in the air fryer basket and bake for 30 minutes at 325°F until firm, but with a slight wobble.

8 Place on a wire rack and let cool completely in the pan, then place in the fridge for at least 1 hour (and up to overnight).

9 Once chilled, release from the pan and slice into wedges.

KEEP IT This pie will keep for up to 5 days in an airtight container.

Prep + cook time
1 hour, plus chilling
Serves 10

CAKES

From indulgent chocolate stout cake to sprinkle-topped baked donuts, your air fryer will bake all manner of baked treats to perfection. You can buy silicone molds that are designed for air fryers, or use small loaf or cake pans that fit—simply bake in batches if needed.

FIERY GINGER CAKE

---

2 eggs
½ cup (120ml) vegetable oil
1¾oz (50g) molasses
¾ cup (150g) dark brown sugar
1¼ cup (150g) all-purpose flour
1 tsp baking powder
1½ tsp salt
2 tsp ground ginger
1 tsp ground cinnamon
1 tsp allspice
1 tsp ground black pepper
1½oz (40g) candied ginger in syrup,
   finely chopped

SYRUP:
juice of 1 orange
juice of 1 lime
1 piece of candied ginger, finely
   diced
50g (¼ cup) dark brown sugar

1 Combine the eggs, oil, molasses, and sugar in a medium mixing bowl, and whisk until fully combined. Sift in the dry ingredients, continuing to whisk until just combined, then fold in the finely chopped ginger.
2 Preheat the air fryer to 325°F for 3 minutes.
3 Pour the cake batter into a greased and parchment paper–lined 8½ x 4½in (21.6 x 11.6 cm) loaf pan, and cook in the preheated air fryer for 40 minutes at 325°F until an inserted skewer comes out clean (if the skewer has wet cake batter on it, continue to bake at 5-minute intervals until the skewer is clean).
4 Remove the pan from the air fryer and let cool on a wire rack while you make the syrup.

5 Place all the syrup ingredients in small pan over medium heat, bring to a gentle simmer, and cook for 5 minutes.
6 Turn out the cooled cake and place on a rimmed plate or in a clean baking sheet. Spoon over the hot syrup, then let cool fully.

KEEP IT Store for up to 5 days in an airtight container.

Prep + cook time
1 hour
Serves 8–10

TIP This can be served as is or toasted and spread with butter.

CHOCOLATE STOUT CAKE WITH CREAM CHEESE FROSTING

1 cup (225g) butter
⅔ cup (60g) unsweetened cocoa
   powder, plus extra to decorate
1 cup (225ml) stout
1 cup (200g) sugar
1 cup (180g) light brown sugar
2 eggs, beaten
¾ cup (150g) plain yogurt
1 tsp vanilla extract
2 cups (250g) all-purpose flour
1 tsp baking soda
1 tsp baking powder

CREAM CHEESE FROSTING:
½ cup plus 2 tbsp (150g) butter,
   softened
2 cups plus 2 tbsp (300g) powdered
   sugar
1 tsp fine salt
1 tsp vanilla extract
1⅓ cups (300g) cream cheese

1 Place the butter in a medium saucepan and melt over low heat. Whisk in the cocoa and stout until you have a lump-free liquid, then remove from heat. Set aside to cool until the mixture is lukewarm.

2 Whisk together the sugars, eggs, yogurt, and vanilla in a large mixing bowl, then pour in the lukewarm butter-cocoa mixture. Whisk again until combined.

3 Sift the flour, baking soda, and baking powder into the batter and whisk until all the flour is absorbed.

4 Preheat the air fryer to 325°F for 3 minutes.

5 Pour the batter into a greased and parchment paper–lined 8–9in (20–23cm) loose-bottomed cake pan. Bake at 325°F for 1 hour.

6 Let cool in the pan on a wire rack for 30 minutes, then turn out and let cool completely.

7 While the cake is cooling, prepare the frosting Beat the softened butter until light, then gradually sift in the powdered sugar, beating until it is fluffy and airy. Stir in the salt and vanilla extract, then finally fold in the cream cheese. Beat until this is fully combined and the frosting is smooth. Place the frosting in the fridge to firm up while the cake continues to cool.

8 Once the cake is cold, place it on a platter or plate, then dollop on the frosting. Smooth it with a spoon, then dust the cake with cocoa to decorate.

KEEP IT This cake will keep for 3 days in an airtight container in the fridge.

Prep + cook time
2 hours
Serves 8–12

TOASTED S'MORES CAKE

1¼ cups (250g) sugar
2 eggs
⅓ cup (90ml) vegetable oil
¾ cup (180g) plain yogurt
1½ tsp vanilla extract
2 cups (250g) all-purpose flour
1 tsp baking powder
1 tsp baking soda
⅔ cup (160ml) boiling water
5¼oz (150g) packaged cookies, crushed, plus extra to decorate
to decorate: marshmallows, edible gold leaf, gold chocolate balls, and indoor sparklers (optional)

CHOCOLATE GANACHE:
1¼ cups (300ml) heavy cream
4 tbsp honey
10½oz (300g) dark chocolate, finely chopped

1 Place the sugar, eggs, oil, yogurt, and vanilla extract into a large mixing bowl. Whisk until combined, then sift in the dry ingredients. Whisk until all the flour is incorporated, then add the boiling water and whisk until you have a runny cake batter. (It may seem odd to pour boiling water into cake mix, but this results in a delicious moist but chewy cake.)

2 Preheat the air fryer to 350°F for 3 minutes.

3 Pour the cake batter into a greased and parchment paper–lined 8in (20cm) round cake pan, then crumble over the crushed cookies. Place the pan in the preheated air fryer and bake for 35 minutes at 350°F until the crust is a deep golden color and an inserted skewer comes out clean.

4 Let cool on a wire rack for 15 minutes, then turn the cake out of the pan and let cool completely.

5 While the cake is cooling, you can make the chocolate ganache. Gently heat the cream in a small saucepan with the honey. Place the chopped chocolate in a medium heatproof bowl. When the cream mixture is steaming hot, pour it over the chocolate. Let it sit for 30 seconds, then stir until all the chocolate has melted.

6 Once the cake has cooled, top with chocolate ganache and decorate with extra crumbled cookies, some marshmallows, edible gold leaf, gold chocolate balls, and indoor sparklers, if you like.

KEEP IT This cake will keep for up to 3 days stored in an airtight container.

Prep + cook time
1 hour
Serves 8–12

ORANGE, FENNEL & POLENTA CAKE
(GLUTEN-FREE)

1 orange
3½oz (100g) olive oil
½ cup (100g) sugar
1 tsp ground fennel seeds
2 eggs, beaten
¼ cup (50g) Greek or plain yogurt
1 cup (150g) cornmeal
¾ cup (80g) ground almonds

1 Start by preparing the orange purée. Pierce the whole orange multiple times with a fork, then place in a small saucepan of water. Bring to a boil and simmer gently for 15 minutes until the orange becomes tender. Remove from the water, place in a blender, and blend to a coarse pulp. Alternatively, if you do not have blender, let the orange cool, then chop into a pulp using a large knife.

2 In a large mixing bowl, combine all the remaining ingredients. Beat with a wooden spoon until you have a smooth batter. Fold in the orange pulp.

3 Preheat the air fryer to 350°F for 3 minutes.

4 Grease 6–8 small ramekins and dust with cornmeal. Fill each ramekin three-quarters full with cake mixture, then bake in the air fryer for 15 minutes at 350°F.

5 Turn out onto a wire rack and let cool for 15 minutes, then either serve warm or let cool completely.

KEEP IT Will keep for up to 5 days in an airtight container.

SERVE IT Serve warm with Greek yogurt and honey.

Prep + cook time
1 hour
Makes 6–8

COCONUT & RASPBERRY LAMINGTONS

½ cup (120g) butter, softened
½ cup plus 4 tsp (120g) sugar
2 eggs
1 tsp vanilla extract
1 tsp salt
1 cup (120g) all-purpose flour
1½ tsp baking powder
2 tbsp raspberry jam

COATING:
3½oz (100g) dark chocolate, finely chopped
2 tbsp (30g) butter
⅔ cup (50g) unsweetened shredded coconut

1 Combine the butter, sugar, eggs, vanilla, and salt in a medium bowl. Beat until combined, then sift in the flour and baking powder. Mix until you have smooth batter.

2 Preheat the air fryer to 325°F for 3 minutes.

3 Divide the cake batter among eight square silicone brownie molds. Bake in the preheated air fryer for 12 minutes at 325°F (you may need to do this in batches) until light golden brown and the cake bounces back when pressed.

4 Remove from the air fryer and let cool on a wire rack in the silicone molds for 5 minutes. While still warm, pop the cake out of the molds, then let cool completely before icing.

5 Meanwhile, for the coating, melt the chopped chocolate and butter in a heatproof bowl over a pan of simmering water. Set aside.

6 Take one cake and place ½ tbsp jam on top, spreading it out to the edges using the back of the spoon. Place a second cake on top. Place the layered cakes back onto the wire rack.

7 Using a pastry brush, cover each cake with the chocolate coating.

8 Place the coconut on a plate, then roll each lamington in coconut until each side is coated.

KEEP IT These will keep for 3 days in an airtight container.

**Prep + cook time
1 hour
Makes 4**

NEAPOLITAN CAKE

1½ cups (300g) plain yogurt
¾ cup (180ml) vegetable oil
3 eggs
1 cup plus 2 tbsp (225g) sugar
1 tsp vanilla extract
1 tsp salt
2¼ cups (300g) all-purpose flour,
    plus 2 tbsp for the strawberry
    sponge
2 tsp baking powder
1 tsp baking soda
2 tbsp unsweetened cocoa powder
½ tsp pink food coloring
6 strawberries, crushed
6 strawberries, sliced
To decorate: chocolate sprinkles,
    wafers, and strawberries

ICING:
½ cup plus 5 tsp (200g) butter,
    softened
3 cups (400g) powdered sugar
1 cup (200g) cream cheese
1 tsp vanilla extract
1 tsp salt
½ tsp pink food coloring

1 Combine the yogurt, oil, eggs, sugar, vanilla, and salt in a bowl. Sift in the flour, baking powder, and baking soda. Whisk until smooth.
2 Divide the batter equally among three bowls. Set one aside. Add the cocoa to the second bowl. To the final bowl, add the coloring, crushed strawberries, and extra 2 tablespoons flour.
3 Preheat the air fryer to 325°F for 3 minutes.
4 Dollop spoonfuls of each cake batter into two greased and parchment paper–lined 8in (20cm) round pans. Using a skewer, swirl the three batters together.
5 Bake each cake in the air fryer for 25 minutes at 325°F until an inserted skewer comes out clean.
6 For the icing, beat the butter in a mixing bowl, gradually adding the powdered sugar, until fluffy. Beat in the cream cheese, vanilla, and salt. Set aside.
7 Remove one-third of the icing and set aside. Add the pink food coloring to the rest and mix well.
8 Once the cakes are baked, place on a wire rack to cool for 15 minutes in their pans, then turn out and let cool completely.
9 Place each buttercream in a piping bag fitted with a star nozzle.
10 Place a layer of cake onto a cake plate, pipe with pink buttercream, then add the sliced strawberries on top. Place the second cake on top, bottom-side down. Pipe the rest of the pink icing in swirls on the top. Pipe swirls of white icing in the gaps, then decorate with chocolate sprinkles, wafers, and strawberries.

KEEP IT Store in an airtight container in the fridge for 3 days.

Cook + prep time
2 hours
Serves 8–12

UPSIDE-DOWN MARMALADE CAKE

⅔ cup (200g) marmalade
¾ cup (180g) butter, softened
1 cup minus 1½ tbsp (180g) sugar
grated zest of 1 orange
3 eggs, beaten
5 tbsp (75ml) kefir
1 tsp sea salt
1⅓ cups (180g) all-purpose flour
1½ tsp baking powder
1 tsp baking soda

1 Spoon the marmalade into the base of a greased 8in (20cm) loose-bottomed round pan, and spread it out to create an even layer using the back of the spoon. Set aside while you make the cake.

2 In a medium mixing bowl, combine the butter, sugar, and orange zest, beating with a wooden spoon for 5 minutes until light and fluffy.

3 Pour the beaten eggs and kefir into the bowl, beat to combine, then sprinkle in the salt and sift in the flour, baking powder, and baking soda. Continue mixing until the batter is a smooth consistency and all the flour is absorbed.

4 Preheat the air fryer to 350°F for 3 minutes.

5 Transfer the cake batter to the pan, then bake in the air fryer for 35–40 minutes at 350°F. The crust should be a deep golden brown and the cake should be firm to touch.

6 Transfer to a wire rack to cool for 20–30 minutes until cool enough to handle, but still warm, then flip it out onto a plate. (The cake needs to be turned out while still warm so that the marmalade doesn't set to the pan.)

KEEP IT Keep for up to 5 days in an airtight container.

Prep + cook time
1 hour
Serves 8

SPICED BROWN SUGAR, LIME & PINEAPPLE LOAF

1 x 8.25oz (233g) can pineapple
 chunks in juice
grated zest and juice of 1 lime
½ tsp chili flakes
¾ cup (140g) light brown sugar
1 stick (120g) butter, softened
grated zest and juice of 1 orange
2 eggs
1 cup (120g) all-purpose flour
1 tsp baking powder
½ tsp salt
¼ cup (50g) sugar

TIP Eat while still warm with a scoop of mango sorbet and grating of lime zest, or let cool and eat simply by the slice with a coffee.

1 Drain the can of pineapple and reserve the juice for the syrup. Place the pineapple chunks, lime zest, chili flakes, and 2 tbsp (20g) brown sugar in a medium bowl, and mix until combined and the sugar has dissolved. Pour the pineapple chunks into a greased 8½ x 4½in (21.6 x 11.6cm) loaf pan and set aside.

2 Combine the butter, orange zest, and remaining brown sugar in a medium mixing bowl, and beat for 5 minutes until the mixture becomes fluffier in texture. Add the eggs, and mix until just combined. Sift in the flour, baking powder, and salt and mix until you have a smooth batter.

3 Preheat the air fryer to 325°F for 3 minutes.

4 Give the pan a little jiggle to distribute the pineapple chunks along the base, then spoon in the batter, and spread it out evenly.

5 Bake in the preheated air fryer for 40 minutes at 325°F.

6 Meanwhile, make the syrup. Combine the reserved pineapple juice, the orange juice, lime juice, and sugar in a small saucepan over high heat for 5 minutes. Let cool.

7 The cake is ready when it has a deep golden brown crust and an inserted skewer comes out clean. Let cool on a wire rack for 10 minutes.

8 Use a skewer or fork to pierce the cake all over. Pour half of the syrup onto the warm cake and let absorb for 10 minutes, then turn the cake out onto a plate and pour over the remaining syrup.

KEEP IT This cake will keep in an airtight container for up to 3 days.

Prep + cook time
1 hour
Serves 8

BAKED DONUTS WITH VANILLA GLAZE

3½oz (100g) vegetable oil
2 eggs
½ cup (100g) sugar
1 tsp vanilla extract
¾ cup (100g) all-purpose flour
1 tsp baking powder
½ tsp salt

VANILLA GLAZE:
¾ cup (100g) powdered sugar
½ tsp vanilla extract
½ tsp ground cinnamon
1 tbsp water

DECORATION:
3 tbsp sprinkles

1 In a large mixing bowl, whisk the oil, eggs, sugar, and vanilla together until combined. Sift in the flour, baking powder, and salt and whisk again until you have a smooth batter.
2 Preheat the air fryer to 350°F for 3 minutes.
3 Fill 12 silicone donut molds three-quarters full with batter. Transfer to the air fryer basket and bake for 8 minutes at 350°F until lightly golden and firm to touch.
4 Remove the baked donuts from the molds and let cool on a wire rack.
5 Meanwhile, make the glaze. Sift the powdered sugar into a bowl, then combine with the vanilla, cinnamon, and water until smooth.

6 One by one, dunk the top of each cooled donut into the glaze, then place back onto the wire rack, and top with sprinkles. Let set for 30 minutes, then serve.

KEEP IT The donuts will keep for up to 5 days in an airtight container.

Prep + cook time
30 minutes
Makes 12

CHERRY & ALMOND CAKE

7 tbsp (100g) butter, softened
½ cup (100g) sugar
grated zest of 1 lemon
2 eggs
¾ cup (80g) ground almonds
⅔ cup (80g) all-purpose flour
¾ tsp baking powder
½ tsp salt
5¼oz (150g) cherries, pitted and halved
1 tbsp cornstarch
3 tbsp cherry jam
8 cherries, to decorate

ICING:
1 cup (150g) powdered sugar
¾oz (25g) cherry jam
juice of ½ lemon

1 Combine the butter, sugar, and lemon zest in a mixing bowl, and beat for 5 minutes until fluffy. Add the eggs and ground almonds, and mix until combined. Sift in the flour, baking powder, and salt, and fold in until just incorporated.
2 In a small bowl, combine the pitted cherries with the cornstarch, and stir until coated. Fold the coated cherries into the batter.
3 Preheat the air fryer to 350°F for 3 minutes.
4 Pour one-quarter of the cake batter into a greased and floured pudding tin, tall cake pan, or tube pan, then top with 1 tablespoon cherry jam, and spread the jam with the back of the spoon. Repeat with two more layers of batter and jam, and finish with a layer of batter. Smooth the surface.
5 Bake in the air fryer for 10 minutes at 350°F.

6 Turn the temperature down to 325°F and cook for 45 minutes until an inserted skewer comes out clean. Do not open the air fryer until the cake has been cooking for at least 35 minutes; otherwise, it may collapse.
7 Let cool in the pan for 30 minutes.
8 Meanwhile, make the icing. Sift the powdered sugar into a bowl, then add the cherry jam and lemon juice. The icing should have a thick consistency and run slowly when you lift up the spoon; add more powdered sugar if needed to thicken.
9 Once the cake has cooled fully, turn it out and cover the top in icing, allowing it to drip down the sides. Top with cherries.

KEEP IT This will keep for up to 3 days in an airtight container.

**Cook + prep time
1 hour 30 minutes
Serves 6–8**

PASTRY

Whether you're making your own pie crust or using sheets of pre-rolled puff pastry, you will find it can be transformed into crispy savory rolls or sweet pies in no time. Phyllo pastry is also featured in this chapter, as the heat of the air fryer crisps it to fabulously flaky perfection.

FENNEL & CHILI SAUSAGE ROLLS

1lb (450g) Italian sausage, casings removed
1 tsp fennel seeds, plus extra to garnish
1 tsp chili flakes
½ tsp garlic powder
1 tsp salt
black pepper, to taste
1 x 11oz (320g) sheet of puff pastry
3½oz (100g) tomato jam
1 egg, beaten
flaked sea salt, to garnish
to serve: chutney (optional)

1 Place the sausage meat in a large bowl. Add the fennel seeds, chili flakes, garlic powder, and salt, and give it a good few twists of black pepper. Use your hands to mix. Set aside.
2 Unroll the puff pastry, keeping it on the sheet of paper. Cut it lengthwise in half. Separate the pieces slightly so you have some room to work.
3 Using a small spoon, spread half of the chutney down the center of each piece of pastry, in a strip about 1in (2.5cm) wide.
4 Take half of the sausage meat and start to form a sausage on the jam. Use your hands to shape it gently; it should be about 1½in (4cm) thick and the whole length of the pastry.
5 Using a pastry brush, brush beaten egg along the bottom edge of pastry. Take the top edge of the pastry and gently lift it over the sausage meat to meet the egg-washed edge.

6 Use your hands to shape the pastry around the meat, ensuring there are no gaps. Crimp along the whole length with a fork and trim off uneven edges. Repeat with second strip of pastry
7 Brush with egg, then garnish with flaked sea salt and fennel seeds. Cut each roll into three pieces.
8 Place the sausage rolls on a parchment paper–lined baking sheet. Chill in the fridge for 15 minutes (or up to overnight).
9 Preheat the air fryer to 350°F for 3 minutes.
10 Place directly into the air fryer basket and bake at 350°F for 16 minutes, or until deep golden. Cool for 10 minutes before serving.

KEEP IT Keep for up to 3 days in an airtight container in the fridge. Warm using the re-heat setting on your air fryer.

**Prep + cook time
45 minutes, plus chilling
Makes 6**

CURRIED POTATO & MANGO CHUTNEY PASTIES

---

1 small onion, finely chopped
1 garlic clove, grated
1in (2.5cm) piece of ginger, peeled
   and finely chopped
½ tsp mustard seeds
1 tsp cumin seeds
½ tsp nigella seeds
1 tsp curry powder
1 tsp sea salt
2 tbsp vegetable oil
12oz (350g) potato, peeled
   and cubed
5 tbsp mango chutney
2 tbsp chopped cilantro
1 egg, beaten
1 tsp nigella seeds
to serve: raita or extra mango
   chutney

PASTRY:
2¼ cups (300g) all-purpose flour,
   plus extra for dusting
½ cup plus 2 tbsp (150g) butter, cold
1 tsp sea salt
3 tbsp cold water

1 Preheat the air fryer to 350°F for 3 minutes.
2 Combine the onion, garlic, ginger, spices, salt, and oil in a heatproof dish. Bake for 10 minutes at 350°F, then add the cubed potato, and bake for another 10 minutes. Stir and bake for a further 10 minutes, then set aside to cool.
3 For the pastry, place the flour in a mixing bowl. Using the largest side on a box grater, grate the cold butter into the bowl. Using your fingers, rub the butter into the flour until it's a sandy consistency. Add the salt and cold water, and knead the pastry until it comes together into a smooth ball. Wrap the pastry in plastic wrap, then flatten into a disc. Chill in the fridge for 30 minutes.
4 Place the chilled pastry on a lightly floured work surface and roll out to ½in (1cm) thick.

5 Cut out a 7in (18cm) pastry circle. Reroll the scraps to cut another circle the same size.
6 Combine the potato filling, mango chutney, and cilantro. Divide between the pastry circles. Pile the filling on the right-hand side of each circle, leaving a 1in (2.5cm) border.
7 Brush the border with beaten egg. Lift the left side of the pastry over the filling. Using a thumb and two fingers, crimp the pastry edge. Brush with egg, then sprinkle with the nigella seeds. Cut a ½in (1cm) hole in the center for steam to escape.
8 Place directly into the air fryer basket and bake for 25 minutes at 350°F, or until deep golden brown. Cool for 10 minutes before serving with raita or extra mango chutney.

Prep + cook time
1 hour, plus chilling
Makes 2

THAI-STYLE SWEET POTATO ROLLS

2 sweet potatoes, peeled and cubed
1 small red onion, finely chopped
1in (2.5cm) piece of ginger, peeled
    and finely chopped
1 stick lemongrass, finely chopped
1 tsp flaked sea salt
2 tsp vegetable oil
grated zest and juice of 1 lime
2 tbsp cilantro, chopped
3 tbsp crunchy peanut butter
⅔ cup (160ml) coconut cream
1 x 11oz (320g) sheet of puff pastry
1 egg, beaten
2 tbsp crushed peanuts
to serve: sweet chili sauce

1 Preheat the air fryer to 350°F for 3 minutes.
2 Combine the sweet potatoes, onion, ginger, lemongrass, salt, and oil in a mixing bowl. Put into a heatproof dish and roast for 15 minutes at 350°F, stirring halfway through, until the sweet potato is soft when pierced with a knife.
3 Pour the filling back into the mixing bowl and mix in the lime zest and juice, cilantro, peanut butter, and coconut cream. Set aside to cool completely.
4 Unroll the sheet of puff pastry, keeping it on the sheet of paper. Cut it in half lengthwise, then divide the filling between the pieces of pastry, placing it down the center of each piece to form a long sausage.
5 Brush egg along the bottom edge of the pastry. Take the top edge of the pastry and gently lift it over the sausage meat to meet the egg-washed edge.

6 Use your hands to shape the pastry around the filling, ensuring there are no gaps. Crimp along the whole length with a fork and trim off uneven edges. Slide the paper onto a baking sheet and chill in the fridge for 15 minutes.
7 Trim off the ends of the rolls and discard. Brush the rolls with beaten egg and sprinkle with the crushed peanuts. Cut each roll into six pieces.
8 Preheat the air fryer to 350°F for 3 minutes.
9 Bake for 12–15 minutes at 350°F, or until deep golden brown and crisp. Let cool for 10 minutes before serving warm with sweet chili sauce for dipping.

KEEP IT They will keep for up to 3 days in the fridge in an airtight container.

Prep + cook time
1 hour, plus chilling
Makes 12

FETA & SPINACH PIE

1lb 5oz (600g) baby spinach
1 leek, thinly sliced
1 tbsp olive oil
grated zest of 1 lemon
1 garlic clove, crushed
4 tbsp finely chopped parsley
4 tbsp finely chopped dill
4 tbsp finely chopped mint
black pepper, to taste
2 eggs, beaten
8oz (225g) feta, crumbled
7 tbsp (100g) butter, melted
1 x 11oz (320g) pack of phyllo pastry,
    defrosted if frozen
2 tsp sesame seeds
2 tsp nigella seeds
flaked sea salt, for sprinkling

TIP You can also use frozen spinach. Defrost it and squeeze out the excess water before using.

1 Cover the spinach in boiling water for 1 minute, then drain and cool. Once cool, squeeze the spinach tightly, draining out excess water. Set aside in a bowl.
2 Preheat the air fryer to 350°F for 3 minutes.
3 Put the leek into a heatproof dish with the oil and a sprinkle of salt. Place in the air fryer and cook at 350°F for 10 minutes, stirring halfway through. Combine with the spinach.
4 Add the lemon zest, garlic, and herbs, and season with black pepper. Add the eggs and combine. Fold in the feta, leaving nice chunks of cheese in the filling. Set aside.
5 Brush melted butter inside a deep 8in (20cm) loose-bottomed pan. Layer half of the phyllo pastry in the pan, brushing each layer generously with butter, and letting the edges overhang the sides of the pan.

6 Add the spinach and feta mixture, then fold in the overhanging pastry edges to cover the filling.
7 Brush a sheet of the remaining pastry with butter, scrunch it up, and place on top of the pie. Repeat with the remaining pastry until the pie is covered. Sprinkle with the seeds and some flaked sea salt.
8 Preheat the air fryer to 350°F for 3 minutes.
9 Place the pie in the preheated air fryer basket and cook at 350°F for 20 minutes. Reduce the heat to 325°F and bake for 20 minutes more.
10 Carefully remove the side of the pan, then place the pie back in the air fryer for 20 minutes to crisp up the sides. Leave to cool for 10 minutes before cutting.

Prep + cook time
1 hour 30 minutes
Serves 6–8

SAUSAGE RAGU PIE

2 shallots, thinly sliced
1 celery stalk, thinly sliced
1 carrot, finely chopped
2 tbsp olive oil
1lb (450g) Italian sausage, casings
　　removed
1 garlic clove, crushed
1 x 14.5oz (400g) can diced tomatoes
3½ tbsp (50ml) red wine
⅓ cup (100ml) water
3½oz (100g) sweet red peppers,
　　roughly chopped
1 bay leaf
3 sprigs of rosemary
1 egg, beaten
flaked sea salt

PIE CRUST PASTRY:
1½ cups (200g) all-purpose flour,
　　plus extra for dusting
7 tbsp (100g) butter, cold
4 tbsp cold water

1 For the pastry, place the flour in a bowl. Using a box grater, grate in the butter. Rub the flour and butter together until you have a chunky crumb. Add the cold water and mix with your hands until the dough forms a shaggy ball.

2 Knead the dough gently on a lightly floured surface for 30 seconds until all the flour is absorbed, but you can still see flecks of butter. Form it into a 1in (2.5cm) thick disc, wrap in plastic wrap, and chill it while you make the filling.

3 Preheat the air fryer to 375°F for 3 minutes.

4 Place the shallots, celery, and carrot in a heatproof dish with the olive oil and a sprinkle of salt. Roast in the air fryer at 375°F for 10 minutes. Stir, then add the sausage and roast for 10 minutes. Use a spoon to break up the meat, then add the garlic, diced tomatoes, and red wine.

5 Use the water to rinse the tomato can and add with the red peppers, the bay leaf, and rosemary. Roast for 40 minutes, stirring halfway through.

6 Spoon the ragu into a 9in (22cm) metal pie pan. Let cool for 30 minutes.

7 Roll out the pastry to a 10in (25cm) disc. Brush the edges of the dish with egg, then add the pastry lid. Press the edges down to seal it to the dish. Trim off any excess and crimp the rim. Brush with egg and sprinkle with flaked salt. Cut a 1¼in (3cm) slit in the lid for steam to escape.

8 Preheat the air fryer to 350°F for 3 minutes.

9 Cook at 350°F for 35–40 minutes until golden brown. Let cool for 10 minutes before serving.

Prep + cook time
2 hours
Serves 4–6

HONEYED FIG & RICOTTA PHYLLO PARCELS

---

6 sheets of phyllo pastry, defrosted
    if frozen
4 tbsp (60g) butter, melted
½ cup (120g) ricotta
4 tbsp fig jam
2 tbsp honey
to serve: figs, honey, and
    toasted nuts

1 Lay out one sheet of phyllo pastry on the work surface, brush generously with melted butter, then fold in half like a book.
2 Dollop one-sixth of the ricotta and jam in the bottom left-hand corner, leaving a 1¼in (3cm) border from the edge of the pastry. Fold the bottom right-hand corner over the filling to create a triangle shape, pressing down the pastry with the edges of your hands to seal the filling inside. Finally, fold the pastry upward to create another layer and then again until you have a triangular parcel.
3 Brush the outside of the parcel with melted butter and set aside. Continue the process until you have all six parcel.

4 Preheat the air fryer to 350°F for 3 minutes.
5 Place the parcels directly in the air fryer basket and bake at 350°F for 12–15 minutes, or until evenly golden brown.
6 Let cool for 5 minutes before serving with fresh figs, a drizzle of honey, and some toasted nuts.

SERVE IT These are best eaten fresh!

Prep + cook time
1 hour
Makes 6

SPICED PUMPKIN PIES

1 cup (225g) pumpkin puree
½ cup (100g) light brown sugar
1 egg
½ tbsp cornstarch
1 tsp ground cinnamon
1 tsp ground ginger
½ tsp allspice
½ tsp ground black pepper
½ tsp salt
to serve: crème fraîche and
   maple syrup

COOKIE CRUMB CRUST:
9oz (250g) crispy caramel cookies,
   crumbled
½ tsp salt
½ cup (120g) butter, melted

1 Place the pumpkin, sugar, egg, cornstarch, cinnamon, ginger, allspice, pepper, and salt into a mixing bowl, then beat with a wooden spoon until fully combined. Set aside while you make the cookie crumb crust.
2 Place the cookies inside a sealed food bag and bash with a rolling pin until they resemble a fine sandy crumb. Alternatively, you can place these into a food processor and pulse. Pour the cookie crumbs into a small mixing bowl, then add the salt and melted butter. Mix well with a spoon until all the crumbs are coated and the butter is absorbed.
3 Divide the cookie crumb mixture among six 4in (10cm) ramekins or small tart shells. Using the back of a small spoon, press the crumbs to create a crust (shell) about ¼in (5mm) thick, pressing it up the sides and into the edges.

4 Preheat the air fryer to 325°F for 3 minutes.
5 Bake at 325°F for 5 minutes.
6 Divide the pumpkin filling evenly among the six dishes. Smooth the top of the pies before placing back in the air fryer and baking for a further 10 minutes at 325°F.
7 Let cool completely on a wire rack, then remove the pies or serve from the ramekin. Serve with a dollop of crème fraîche and a drizzle of maple syrup.

KEEP IT These will keep for up to 3 days in the fridge.

Prep + cook time
30 minutes
Makes 6

PISTACHIO & ORANGE BLOSSOM BAKLAVA

1⅔ cup (200g) pistachios, plus extra
    crushed pistachios to decorate
¾ cup (100g) pecans or walnuts
2¼ tbsp (40g) honey
grated zest of 1 orange
1 tsp sea salt
7oz (200g) butter, melted
9½oz (270g) phyllo pastry sheets,
    defrosted if frozen

SYRUP:
¾ cup (150g) sugar
juice of 1 orange
1 tsp ground cinnamon

TIP The baklava can be eaten immediately once cool but is best left to set overnight in the fridge.

1 Place all the nuts in a food processor and pulse to a coarse sand. Place in a mixing bowl with the honey, orange zest, and sea salt. Mix and set aside.
2 Brush a 20cm (8in) brownie tin with melted butter. Brush a sheet of pastry edge to edge with butter. Lay it in the tin, pressing it into the corners. Butter another sheet and layer the opposite way. Repeat the process, alternating layers, until you've used six sheets.
3 Fill the lined tin with the nut filling, pressing the filling down until it's compacted. Using scissors, trim off any overhanging pastry and fold over any extra edges inwards.
4 Cut the remaining sheets of filo pastry into 20cm (8in) squares. Brush each sheet with butter and layer on top of the nut filling, pressing down firmly.
5 Brush the top layer with the remaining butter.

6 Take a small sharp knife and score six diagonal lines into the pastry, then six vertical lines to create the classic diamond shape.
7 Preheat the air fryer to 160°C/325°F for 3 minutes.
8 Put in the air fryer basket and bake at 160°C/325°F for 10 minutes, then cover with foil and cook at 140°C/280°F for 25 minutes.
9 Meanwhile, combine the syrup ingredients and 3½ tablespoons water in a small pan, bring to a simmer, and cook for 5 minutes until it coats the back of a spoon.
10 While hot, cover the baklava with the syrup. Top with extra crushed pistachios and place on a wire rack to cool completely in the tin.

KEEP IT This will keep for up to 2 weeks in an airtight container.

Prep + cook time
1 hour, plus setting
Serves 18

PLUM & BLACKBERRY PIES

8 ripe plums
1 cup (150g) blackberries
grated zest and juice of 1 lemon
½ cup (100g) cane sugar
1 tbsp cornstarch
1 egg, beaten
2 tbsp sugar
to serve: whipped cream

PASTRY:
½ cup (120g) butter, softened
½ cup plus 1 tbsp (80g) powdered
    sugar
1 egg, beaten
½ tsp vanilla extract
½ tsp salt
1½ cups (200g) all-purpose flour,
    plus extra for dusting

1 Preheat the air fryer to 400°F for 3 minutes.
2 Pit then cut each plum into sixths. Put in a bowl with the blackberries, lemon zest and juice, sugar, and cornstarch, and combine. Transfer to a heatproof dish.
3 Place in the air fryer and bake at 400°F for 15 minutes, stirring every 5 minutes. Cover with plastic wrap to prevent a skin from forming.
4 To make the pastry, in a mixing bowl, beat the softened butter with the powdered sugar, then add the egg, vanilla, and salt, and stir until combined. Sift in the flour and stir until a soft dough forms and the flour is absorbed. Wrap in plastic wrap, flatten into a disc, and place in the fridge to chill for 1 hour. At the same time, place the cooled fruit filling in the fridge to chill fully, too.
5 On a floured surface, roll out the pastry to ½in (1cm)
thick. Cut out 12 discs with a 4in (10cm) round cutter. Put on a parchment paper–lined baking sheet and chill for 15 minutes.
6 Divide the filling among six of the discs, piling it in a mound. Brush the edges with egg, then place another disc of pastry on top. Using a flour-dusted fork, seal the edges. Use the pastry ring to trim off any scraggly edges.
7 Brush with egg, sprinkle with the sugar, and cut a ½in (1cm) hole in the top for steam to escape.
8 Preheat the air fryer to 350°F for 3 minutes and line the basket with parchment paper.
9 Put the pastries in the lined basket and bake for 25 minutes until golden.
10 Let cool for 10 minutes before serving with whipped cream.

Prep + cook time
2 hours
Makes 6

PEAR & GINGER STRUDEL

1 lb 2 oz (500g) pears, cored and cubed

1¾ oz (50g) candied ginger, finely chopped

¼ cup (50g) cane sugar

¼ cup (40g) raisins

1 tsp ground cinnamon

2 tbsp (30g) butter, softened, plus 5 tbsp (75g), melted

¾ cup (40g) bread crumbs

6 sheets of phyllo pastry, defrosted if frozen

to serve: powdered sugar and ice cream

1 Preheat the air fryer to 350°F for 3 minutes.

2 Combine the pears, ginger, sugar, raisins, cinnamon, and 1½ tbsp (20g) butter in a mixing bowl. Pour into a heatproof dish and bake at 350°F for 10 minutes, stirring halfway through. Set aside to cool on a wire rack.

3 Turn the heat up to 400°F. Combine the bread crumbs and ½ tbsp (10g) butter in a heatproof dish, and bake at 400°F stirring every minute until evenly golden. Set aside to cool on a wire rack.

4 Take one sheet of pastry and brush with melted butter. Take another sheet and layer 4in (10cm) of it over the buttered sheet to create one longer length. Brush generously with butter, then layer another sheet over the first piece, then another over the second until you've used all six sheets.

5 Combine the filling with the bread crumbs. Spoon the filling in a sausage-like length, 4in (10cm) from the top edge of the pastry, leaving 2in (5cm) of pastry at each end. Fold the ends of the pastry inward to encase the filling. Taking the top edge of the pastry, roll downward to create a long sausage. Then roll the pastry into a swirl.

6 Preheat the air fryer to 350°F for 3 minutes.

7 Put the swirl into a greased 8in (20cm) round pan. Brush with any remaining melted butter and bake at 350°F for 25–35 minutes until golden brown.

8 Let cool for 15 minutes, then remove from the pan. Dust with powdered sugar and serve with ice cream.

KEEP IT It keeps for 5 days in an airtight container in the fridge.

Prep + cook time
1 hour
Serves 8

APPLE PIES

4 firm apples, like Granny Smith,
   peeled and cubed
juice of 1 lemon
½ cup (100g) sugar
1½ tbsp cornstarch
2 tbsp (30g) butter, softened
2 tsp ground cinnamon
4 tbsp granulated sugar
1 x 11oz (320g) sheet of puff pastry
all-purpose flour, for dusting
1 egg, beaten

1 Preheat the air fryer to 325°F for 3 minutes.
2 Combine the apples, lemon juice, sugar, cornstarch, butter, and 1 teaspoon cinnamon in a heatproof dish.
3 Place in the air fryer basket and bake at 325°F for 10 minutes, stirring halfway through. Turn the setting up to 400°F for 5 minutes to activate the cornstarch and thicken the filling, stirring again halfway through and again at the end. Remove and cover the filling with plastic wrap to prevent a skin from forming, and place on a wire rack to cool completely.
4 While the filling is cooling, combine the remaining 1 teaspoon cinnamon with the sugar in a small bowl; set aside.
5 Unroll the pastry on a lightly floured work surface. Cut it into eight equal rectangles.

6 Divide the filling among four of the pastry pieces, spooning it into the center of each rectangle and leaving a ¾in (2cm) border around the edge. Brush the border with egg, then top with another rectangle of pastry, gently placing it on top, stretching it over the filling and sealing it using the sides of your hands.
7 Crimp the edges with a fork, then trim with a knife. Cut a ½in (1cm) slit in the center to allow steam to escape. Brush all over with beaten egg and sprinkle with the cinnamon sugar.
8 Preheat the air fryer to 350°F for 3 minutes and line the basket with parchment paper.
9 Bake two pies at a time at 350°F for 16–20 minutes until crisp and golden. Let cool for 10 minutes before serving.

Prep + cook time
1 hour
Makes 4

DOUGHS

There is no getting away from the fact that making dough can be time-consuming. However, once you've made your dough and let it rise, cooking it in an air fryer means your springy breads and sweet, sticky rolls can be ready to enjoy in much less time than when using an oven.

HOT DOG ROLLS WITH MUSTARD MAYO DIP

1½ tsp active dried yeast
⅔ cup (150ml) whole milk, lukewarm, plus extra for brushing
2 cups plus 2 tbsp (300g) bread flour, plus extra for dusting
2 tsp sugar
1 tsp salt
1 egg, beaten
3½ tbsp (50g) butter, softened
15oz (420g) hot dogs
4 large pickle slices, cut in half lengthwise
1 tbsp poppy seeds

DIP:
1 small shallot, finely chopped
5 tbsp mayonnaise
2 tsp spicy mustard
1 tsp tomato ketchup
1 tsp horseradish
1 tbsp roughly chopped dill
½ tsp ground black pepper

1 Sprinkle the yeast over the lukewarm milk. Let sit for 2 minutes until foaming.
2 Add the flour, sugar, and salt into a mixing bowl or a stand mixer fitted with a dough hook. Add the egg and yeasted milk. Stir until a dough starts to form.
3 Knead for 6 minutes, then add the butter, and knead for 5 minutes until smooth and elastic. Put into an oiled bowl, cover with plastic wrap, and set in a warm place for 1–2 hours until doubled in size.
4 Knead on a floured surface for 1 minute, then split the dough into eight portions, 2½oz (70g) each. Roll each portion of dough into a ball. Cover the other balls with a dish towel while you work.
5 Cut eight 4in (10cm) squares of parchment paper. Dust each dough ball with flour and roll into a rectangle, the length of the hot dogs and 3¼in (8cm) wide.

6 Place a halved pickle slice and a hot dog in the center of each piece of dough, then pinch the dough together. Place on a square of parchment paper and then onto a baking sheet. Cover with a towel and let rise for 30 minutes, or until doubled in size.
7 Preheat the air fryer to 350°F for 3 minutes.
8 Brush the rolls with milk and sprinkle with the poppy seeds. Use the parchment paper to lift them into the preheated air fryer. Bake at 350°F for 12 minutes, or until a deep golden brown.
9 Meanwhile, make the dip by combining all the ingredients in a bowl and seasoning to taste.
10 Serve the warm hot dog rolls with the dip!

KEEP IT Store in an airtight container in the fridge for 3 days. Reheat in the air fryer.

Prep + cook time
3 hours
Makes 8

CHEESY GARLIC DOUGH BALLS

1½ tsp active dried yeast
½ cup plus 2 tsp (130ml) whole milk, lukewarm
1¾ cups (250g) bread flour, plus extra for dusting
2 tsp sugar
1 tsp salt
1 egg, beaten
3 tbsp (40g) butter, softened
½ cup (20g) panko bread crumbs
5½oz (150g) grated mozzarella

GARLIC BUTTER:
7 tbsp (100g) butter, softened
4 garlic cloves, minced
2 tbsp roughly chopped parsley

1 Sprinkle the yeast over the lukewarm milk. Let sit for 2 minutes until foaming.
2 Add the flour, sugar, and salt into a mixing bowl or stand mixer with a dough hook. Add the beaten egg and yeasted milk. Combine with a wooden spoon until a dough starts to form.
3 Knead for 6 minutes, then add the softened butter and knead for a further 5 minutes until smooth and elastic. Put into an oiled bowl, cover with plastic wrap, and set in a warm place for 1–2 hours, or until doubled in size.
4 Meanwhile, grease the inside of an 8in (20cm) round pan with butter, then coat with the bread crumbs.
5 Mix together the garlic butter ingredients to combine, then set aside.
6 Knead the dough for 1 minute, then weigh it out into 18 portions, about 1oz (30g) each.

7 Roll each portion into a dough ball, by rolling the dough in circular motions on the work surface.
8 Place all the dough balls into the bread-crumbed pan, leaving a ½in (1cm) gap between them. Sprinkle the grated mozzarella between all the gaps. Cover with plastic wrap and let rise for 30–45 minutes, or until doubled in size.
9 Preheat the air fryer to 350°F for 3 minutes.
10 Place into the preheated air fryer basket and bake for 20 minutes at 350°F until deep golden brown.
11 Melt the garlic parsley butter and brush it over the dough balls, then serve immediately.

**Prep + cook time
3 hours
Makes 18**

CHORIZO, PEPPER & MANCHEGO FOCACCIA

2 tsp active dried yeast
1¼ cups (300ml) lukewarm water
350g (2½ cups) bread flour, plus
   extra for dusting
2 tsp sugar
1 tsp salt
4 tbsp extra-virgin olive oil
3½oz (100g) chorizo, chopped
2½oz (80g) guindilla peppers
1 tsp flaked sea salt
½ cup (50g) grated Manchego
   or Parmesan cheese

1 Sprinkle the yeast over the lukewarm water. Let sit for 2 minutes until foaming.
2 Place the flour, sugar, and salt in a mixing bowl or a stand mixer fitted with a dough hook. Add the yeasted water, and stir with a wooden spoon until a shaggy dough forms.
3 Knead the dough for 5–8 minutes until the dough becomes smooth and elastic. Place in an oiled bowl, cover with plastic wrap, and set aside in a warm spot for 1 hour, or until doubled in size.
4 Once the dough has doubled in sized, turn it out onto a lightly floured work surface and knead for 1 minute to knock out the air.
5 Lightly oil your hands and a deep 8in (20cm) pan, then transfer the dough to the pan. Stretch the dough to fill three-quarters of the pan. Cover and set aside again for 1 hour, or until doubled in size.

6 The dough should be bubbly and jiggle when the pan is gently shaken. Drizzle with 3 tablespoons olive oil, then dimple the dough all over using your oiled fingertips. Sprinkle with the chopped chorizo, guindilla peppers, and flaked sea salt.
7 Preheat the air fryer to 00°F for 3 minutes.
8 Place in the preheated air fryer basket and cook at 400°F for 15–18 minutes, or until the crust is golden brown.
9 Let cool for 15 minutes before removing from the pan to cool completely.
10 Place the focaccia on a board, then sprinkle all over with the grated cheese, and drizzle over the remaining olive oil. Serve in thick slices.

KEEP IT It will keep for up to 3 days in an airtight container.

Prep + cook time
2 hours 45 minutes
Serves 6

MOZZARELLA & MEATBALL CALZONES

¼ tsp active dried yeast
⅔–¾ cup (150–175m) lukewarm water
1¾ cups (250g) bread flour, plus extra for dusting
½ tsp sugar
½ tsp salt

FILLING:
1 shallot, finely chopped
12 small meatballs
2 tbsp olive oil, plus extra for drizzling
½ tsp fine sea salt
½ tsp ground black pepper
1 cup (225ml) pasta sauce
1 garlic clove, finely chopped
1 sprig of basil
1 cup (100g) grated mozzarella

1 Sprinkle the yeast over the lukewarm water. Let sit for 2 minutes until foaming.
2 Place the flour, sugar, and salt in a large mixing bowl or a stand mixer with a dough hook. Add the yeasted water, and stir with a wooden spoon until a shaggy dough forms.
3 Knead for 5–8 minutes until smooth and elastic. Place in an oiled bowl, cover with plastic wrap, and set aside in a warm spot for 1 hour (it will rise a bit, but not double in size).
4 Preheat the air fryer to 400°F for 3 minutes.
5 For the filling, combine the shallot, meatballs, oil, and seasoning in a heatproof dish. Bake in the air fryer at 400°F for 5 minutes. Stir in the pasta sauce and garlic, then submerge the basil in the sauce. Bake for 10 minutes at 350°F, then place on a wire rack to cool.

6 Once the meatballs are cool and the dough has risen, on a floured surface, cut the dough into four pieces. Roll each piece into a 6in (15cm) circle.
7 Place three meatballs, a tablespoon of sauce, and one-quarter of the mozzarella in the center of each circle. Lift the two edges to meet in the middle, then pinch all the way along to seal in the filling. Cut a ½in (1cm) slit in the center to allow steam to escape.
8 Preheat the air fryer to 350°F for 3 minutes.
9 Put in the air fryer basket, drizzle with olive oil, then bake at 350°F for 12 minutes, or until golden brown. Let cool in the basket for a few minutes, then cool on a wire rack for 10 minutes before serving.

Prep + cook time
2 hours
Makes 4

FETA & HOT HONEY SWIRLS

½ tsp active dried yeast
½ cup plus 2 tsp (130ml) whole milk, lukewarm, plus extra for brushing
1¾ cups (250g) bread flour, plus extra for dusting
2 tsp sugar
1 tsp sea salt
1 egg, beaten
3 tbsp (40g) butter, softened
3½oz (100g) feta, crumbled

SPICED BUTTER:
7 tbsp (100g) butter, softened
4 tsp (20g) honey
1 tsp chili flakes
1 tsp dried oregano
1 tsp dried thyme
1 tsp sea salt
1 tsp ground black pepper

1 Sprinkle the yeast over the lukewarm milk. Let sit for 2 minutes until foaming.
2 Place the flour, sugar, and salt in a large mixing bowl or a stand mixer with a dough hook. Add the yeasted milk and beaten egg, and stir with a wooden spoon until a dough forms.
3 Knead for 6 minutes, then add the butter and knead for 5 minutes until smooth and elastic. Place in an oiled bowl, cover with plastic wrap, and set aside in a warm spot for 1 hour, or until doubled in size.
4 Meanwhile, combine the spiced butter ingredients, and set aside.
5 Knead the dough for 1 minute to knock out the air. Dust lightly with flour, then roll out into a 12 x 8in (30 x 20cm) rectangle.
6 Spread two-thirds of the spiced butter on the dough, spreading it from edge to edge, using the back of a spoon, then sprinkle over the crumbled feta.

7 Taking a long edge of the dough, roll it into a tight swirl. Cut it into six equal pieces. Place each piece, swirl-side down, in a small greased ramekin.
8 Place the ramekins on a baking sheet and cover again with plastic wrap. Set aside for 30 minutes to rise in a warm place, or until doubled in size.
9 Preheat the air fryer to 350°F for 3 minutes.
10 Brush the swirls with milk, then place in the air fryer basket and bake for 12 minutes at 350°F, or until a deep golden brown.
11 Brush with the rest of the butter and place on a wire rack to cool in the ramekins for 10 minutes, then turn out and serve warm.

KEEP IT These will keep for up to 3 days in an airtight container in the fridge.

**Prep + cook time
2 hours
Makes 6**

CHOCOLATE ORANGE BABKA

2 tsp active dried yeast
¾ cup (175ml) whole milk, lukewarm, plus extra for brushing
3 cups (400g) all-purpose flour, plus extra for dusting
5 tsp (20g) sugar
grated zest of 1 large orange
1 tsp salt
2 eggs
2 tbsp (30g) butter, softened
½ tsp salt

FILLING:
¼ cup (60g) butter
3½oz (100g) dark chocolate, chopped
4 tbsp unsweetened cocoa powder
2½ tbsp (30g) light brown sugar

SYRUP:
6½ tbsp (80g) sugar
juice of 1 large orange
3½ tbsp water

1 Sprinkle the yeast over the lukewarm milk. Let sit for 2 minutes until foaming.
2 Add the flour, sugar, zest, and salt into a mixing bowl or stand mixer with a dough hook. Add the egg and yeasted milk, and stir with a wooden spoon until a dough starts to form.
3 Knead for 6 minutes, then add the butter and knead for 5 minutes until smooth and elastic. Put into an oiled bowl, cover with plastic wrap, and set in a warm place for 1–2 hours until doubled in size.
4 Meanwhile, put the filling ingredients into a small pan over a low heat and stir until melted. Set aside.
5 Put the syrup ingredients into a small pan and simmer on medium heat for 10 minutes until it coats the spoon. Set aside.
6 Knead the dough for 1 minute, then roll out on a floured surface into a 12 x 10in (30 x 25cm) rectangle.

7 Spread the chocolate filling from edge to edge, coating the whole piece of dough. Taking a long edge, roll it into a tight swirl. Cut the roll in half lengthwise into two long pieces.
8 Place the two pieces next to each other, cut-side up and overlap them like a plait (braid). Gently lift the plait into a greased 8in (20cm) loose-bottomed pan, cut-side up. Cover with plastic wrap and set in a warm place for 1–2 hours until doubled in size.
9 Preheat the air fryer to 340°F for 3 minutes.
10 Brush the dough with milk, put in the preheated air fryer basket, and cook at 340°F for 30 minutes until golden.
11 Brush with the orange syrup while hot. Cool completely in the pan.

**Prep + cook time
3 hours
Serves 8–10**

TAHINI, MAPLE & PECAN BUNS

1½ tsp active dried yeast
½ cup plus 2 tsp (130ml) whole milk, lukewarm
1¾ cups (250g) bread flour, plus extra for dusting
5 tsp (20g) sugar
grated zest of 1 lime, plus extra to decorate
½ tsp salt
1 egg, beaten
3 tbsp (40g) butter, softened

FILLING:
3½ tbsp (50g) butter, softened
2 tbsp (25g) brown sugar
¼ cup (50g) tahini
1¼ tbsp (25g) maple syrup
¾ cup (75g) pecan halves, roughly chopped, plus extra to decorate
1 tsp flaked sea salt

ICING:
¾ cup (100g) powdered sugar
1¼ tbsp (25g) maple syrup
juice of 1 lime

1 Sprinkle the yeast over the lukewarm milk. Let sit for 2 minutes until foaming.
2 Add the flour, sugar, lime zest, and salt into a mixing bowl or stand mixer with a dough hook. Add the egg and yeasted milk. Combine with a wooden spoon until a dough starts to form.
3 Knead for 6 minutes, then add the butter and knead for 5 minutes until smooth and elastic. Put into an oiled bowl, cover with plastic wrap, and set in a warm place for 1–2 hours until doubled in size.
4 Meanwhile, for the filling, place the softened butter, sugar, tahini, and maple syrup in a mixing bowl, and beat until combined. Set aside at room temperature (you want the filling to be spreadable, so don't put it in the fridge).
5 Once risen, knead the dough on a lightly floured work surface for 1 minute. Roll out into a 12 x 10in (30 x 25cm) rectangle.

6 Spread the soft butter filling from edge to edge, then sprinkle with the pecans and sea salt.
7 Taking a long edge of the dough, roll it into a tight swirl. Cut it into six equal pieces. Place each piece, swirl-side down, in a greased baking pan. Set aside to prove for 30 minutes, or until doubled in size.
8 Preheat the air fryer to 350°F for 3 minutes.
9 Place the buns in the air fryer basket and bake at 350°F for 12 minutes until deep golden.
10 For the icing, sift the powdered sugar into a bowl, and stir in the maple syrup and lime juice until smooth.
11 Brush the buns all over with the icing while still warm, then sprinkle with extra pecans and lime zest to decorate.

**Prep + cook time
2 hours 30 minutes
Makes 6**

LEMON CURD & POPPY SEED SWIRLS

1½ tsp active dried yeast
½ cup plus 2 tsp (130ml) whole milk, lukewarm
1¾ cups (250g) bread flour, plus extra for dusting
5 tsp (20g) sugar
grated zest of 1 lemon
3 tbsp poppy seeds
½ tsp salt
1 egg, beaten
3 tbsp (40g) butter, softened
5½oz (150g) lemon curd

ICING:
¾ cup (100g) powdered sugar, sifted
juice of 1 lemon
1 tbsp poppy seeds

1 Sprinkle the yeast over the lukewarm milk. Let sit for 2 minutes until foaming.
2 Add the flour, sugar, lemon zest, poppy seeds, and salt into a mixing bowl or stand mixer with a dough hook. Add the egg and yeasted milk. Combine with a wooden spoon until a dough starts to form.
3 Knead for 6 minutes, then add the butter and knead for 5 minutes until smooth and elastic. Put into an oiled bowl, cover with plastic wrap, and set in a warm place for 1–2 hours until doubled in size.
4 Once risen, knead the dough on a lightly floured work surface for 1 minute. Roll out into a 12 x 10in (30 x 25cm) rectangle.
5 Spread the lemon curd from edge to edge over the whole piece of dough.
6 Taking a long edge of the dough, roll it into a tight swirl. Cut the swirl into six equal pieces.

7 Place each piece, swirl-side down, in a greased baking pan.
8 Cover with plastic wrap and let rise for 30 minutes, or until doubled in size.
9 Once risen, preheat the air fryer to 350°F for 3 minutes.
10 Place the buns in the preheated air fryer and cook at 350°F for 12 minutes.
11 Meanwhile, combine the icing ingredients in a bowl and mix until smooth.
12 Remove the buns from the air fryer and let cool for 5 minutes, then brush generously with icing while still warm.

KEEP IT Keep for up to 3 days in an airtight container.

**Prep + cook time
2 hours 30 minutes
Makes 6**

APPLE CRUMBLE BUNS

½ tsp active dried yeast
½ cup plus 2 tsp (130ml) whole milk, lukewarm, plus extra for brushing
1¾ cups (250g) bread flour, plus extra for dusting
1 tsp ground cinnamon
5 tsp (20g) sugar
½ tsp sea salt
1 egg, beaten
1 tsp vanilla extract
3 tbsp (40g) butter, softened

FILLING:
2 apples, peeled, cored, and cut into ¼in (5mm) chunks
1½ tbsp (20g) butter
1 tbsp sugar
1 tsp ground cinnamon
⅔ cup (150ml) premade custard

CRUMBLE:
2 tbsp (30g) butter, cold and cubed
5 tbsp (40g) all-purpose flour
5 tsp (20g) sugar
1 tsp flaked sea salt

1 Sprinkle the yeast over the lukewarm milk. Let sit for 2 minutes until foaming.
2 Put the flour, cinnamon, sugar, and salt in a mixing bowl or a stand mixer with a dough hook. Add the egg, vanilla, and yeasted milk. Stir with a wooden spoon until a dough forms.
3 Knead for 6 minutes, add the butter, and knead for 5 minutes until smooth and elastic. Place in an oiled bowl, cover with plastic wrap, and set aside for 1 hour until doubled in size.
4 Preheat the air fryer to 350°F for 3 minutes.
5 For the filling, mix the apples, butter, sugar, and cinnamon in a heatproof dish. Place in the air fryer basket and bake at 350°F for 10–15 minutes until softened and starting to caramelize. Let cool.
6 For the crumble, rub the cold butter into the flour using your fingertips until it is a sandy consistency. Stir in the sugar and salt. Set aside.

7 Cut six 4in (10cm) squares of parchment paper.
8 Knead the dough for 1 minute, then divide into six pieces, and shape into balls. Place each ball onto a square of parchment paper. Lightly dust with flour, then flatten the balls and press a dip in the center using your fingers. Fill each dip with 1 tablespoon custard.
9 Place on a baking sheet, cover with oiled plastic wrap, and let rise 30 minutes until doubled.
10 Preheat the air fryer to 350°F for 3 minutes.
11 Brush with milk, then divide the filling among the buns. Sprinkle with the crumble. Place in the air fryer basket using the paper, and bake for 10 minutes at 350°F until golden brown.
12 Let cool before serving.

Prep + cook time
2 hours 30 minutes
Makes 6

CINNAMON BUNS

½ tsp active dried yeast
⅔ cup (150ml) oat milk or
 alternative, lukewarm
1¾ cups (250g) bread flour, plus
 extra for dusting
5 tsp (20g) sugar
½ tsp sea salt
4 tbsp (60g) butter, softened

FILLING:
7 tbsp (100g) butter, softened
½ cup (100g) light brown sugar
1 tbsp ground cinnamon
1 tsp flaked sea salt

ICING:
1½ cups (200g) powdered sugar
juice of 1 lemon
1 tsp ground cinnamon

1 Sprinkle the yeast over the lukewarm milk. Let sit for 2 minutes until foaming.
2 Place the flour, sugar, and salt in a mixing bowl or a stand mixer fitted with a dough hook. Add the yeasted milk and stir with a wooden spoon until a shaggy dough forms.
3 Knead for 6 minutes, then add the butter and knead for 5 minutes until smooth and elastic. Place in an oiled bowl, cover with plastic wrap, and set aside in a warm spot for 1 hour, or until doubled in size.
4 Meanwhile, combine all the filling ingredients in a small bowl to make the cinnamon butter. Set aside.
5 For the icing, sift the powdered sugar into a bowl, then stir in the lemon juice and cinnamon until smooth and thick.
6 Turn the dough out onto a lightly floured work surface and knead for 1 minute to knock out the air.

7 Roll out into a 12 x 8in (30 x 20cm) rectangle. Spread the cinnamon butter from edge to edge over the whole piece of dough.
8 Taking a long edge of the dough, roll it into a tight swirl. Cut the swirl into four equal pieces.
9 Place the buns swirl-side down in small greased ramekins.
10 Preheat the air fryer to 350°F for 3 minutes.
11 Bake the buns in the preheated air fryer basket for 10–12 minutes at 350°F until deep golden brown, but with a soft doughy center.
12 Cool in the ramekins on a wire rack for 10 minutes, then flip out of the ramekins while still warm and brush generously with the icing. Let cool for another 10 minutes, then enjoy while still warm.

Prep + cook time
2 hours
Makes 4

PISTACHIO & ROSE BUNS

½ tsp active dried yeast
½ cup plus 2 tsp (130ml) whole milk, lukewarm, plus extra for brushing
1¾ cups (250g) bread flour, plus extra for dusting
½ tsp ground cardamom
grated zest of 1 large orange
½ tsp sea salt
1 egg, beaten
4 tsp (20g) honey
3 tbsp (40g) butter, softened

FILLING:
¾ cup (100g) pistachios, plus extra pistachios, chopped, to decorate
6 tbsp (75g) butter, softened
2½ tbsp (40g) honey
1 tsp flaked sea salt

GLAZE:
juice of 1 large orange
2½ tbsp (30g) sugar
½ tbsp dried rose petals, or 2 tsp rose water

1 Sprinkle the yeast over the lukewarm milk. Let sit for 2 minutes until foaming.
2 Place the flour in a large bowl or a stand mixer fitted with a dough hook. Add the cardamom, orange zest, and salt, and mix for 30 seconds until combined. Add the yeasted milk, beaten egg, and honey. Mix with a wooden spoon until a dough starts to form.
3 Knead for 6 minutes, add the butter, and knead for 5 minutes until smooth and elastic. Put into an oiled bowl, cover with plastic wrap, and set in a warm spot for 1 hour until doubled in size.
4 Meanwhile, for the filling, grind the pistachios in a food processor or blender until like coarse sand, then combine with the butter, honey, and salt. Set aside.
5 Mix the glaze ingredients and 2 tablespoons water in a pan. Simmer for 5 minutes until it coats the back of a spoon.

6 Knead the dough for 1 minute, then roll out into a 16 x 8in (40 x 20cm) rectangle. Spread the pistachio butter from edge to edge.
7 Taking a long edge of the dough, roll it into a tight swirl. Cut it into six equal pieces and place in a greased 8in (20cm) square pan, leaving 1in (2.5cm) between each bun.
8 Cover with plastic wrap and set in a warm place for 30 minutes, or until doubled in size.
9 Preheat the air fryer to 350°F for 3 minutes.
10 Brush the buns with milk, then bake in the preheated air fryer at 350°F for 12 minutes until golden.
11 Let cool on a wire rack for 10 minutes, then brush with the glaze and sprinkle with chopped pistachios. Let cool.

**Prep + cook time
2 hours 15 minutes
Makes 6**

DESSERTS

Use your air fryer for fuss-free
desserts, saving yourself time and
energy when you want to whip up a
treat. The efficient heat of the air fryer
creates wonderfully crisp crumble
and cobbler toppings, but you can
even bake meringues to perfection
by using a lower temperature.

MANGO & LIME CHEESECAKE

2⅔ cups (600g) cream cheese
½ cup plus 2 tbsp (125g) sugar
2 tbsp cornstarch
1 egg
⅔ cup (150ml) heavy cream
grated zest of 1 lime, plus extra
   to decorate

CRUST:
6½oz (180g) graham cracker crumbs
6 tbsp (80g) butter, melted

MANGO JELLY:
2 sheets of gelatine
1 x 15 oz (425g) can diced mango in
   syrup, drained with 2 tbsp of syrup
   retained

1 For the crust, combine the graham cracker crumbs and melted butter, then press into a 8in (20cm) round loose-bottom pan in an even layer. Place in the fridge while you make the filling.

2 Whisk the cream cheese, sugar, cornstarch, and egg in a mixing bowl until smooth. Add the cream and lime zest, then whisk again until it is the consistency of softly whipped cream.

3 Preheat the air fryer to 325°F for 3 minutes.

4 Pour the filling on top of the crust, smooth with the back of a spoon, then tap the pan on the work surface to knock out any air bubbles. Place in the air fryer basket and bake at 325°F for 35 minutes until it has a light golden top, is firm, but still has a wobble.

5 Cool completely in the pan on a wire rack, then put in the fridge for at least 2 hours.

6 Once the cheesecake is chilled, you can make the topping. Soak the gelatine in cold water and set aside.

7 Put the drained mango and the syrup into a blender, and blend to a purée. Heat in a small pan over a low heat for 1–2 minutes until just hot (you should be able to touch it; if you overheat the purée, let it cool a little).

8 Remove the softened gelatine sheets from the cold water and place in the warmed purée. Stir to dissolve, then set aside to cool for 10 minutes.

9 Once cool, pour on top of the cheesecake. Chill in the fridge overnight.

10 To help the cheesecake out of the pan, soak a cloth in hot water and apply to the sides of the pan. Push the base out, then slide the cheesecake onto a plate. Decorate with lime zest.

**Prep + cook time
1 hour, plus chilling
Serves 6–8**

SAUCY SALTED CARAMEL CAKES

½ cup plus 2 tbsp (140g) butter,
  softened
¾ cup (140g) dark brown sugar
2 eggs, beaten
1 tsp vanilla extract
1 tsp fine salt
1 cup (140g) all-purpose flour, plus
  extra for dusting
2 tbsp salted caramel sauce
to serve: salted caramel ice cream

1 Combine the softened butter and sugar in a medium mixing bowl, and beat with a wooden spoon until the mixture lightens. Add the eggs, vanilla, and salt, and beat for a minute, then sift in the flour. Fold the flour through until the batter is smooth.
2 Preheat the air fryer to 350°F for 3 minutes.
3 Grease four ramekins and dust with flour. Divide half of the mixture among the ramekins, smoothing it with the back of a spoon to create a flat layer. Create a dip in the center for the caramel sauce to sit in.

4 Spoon ½ tablespoon caramel sauce into each ramekin. Divide the remaining batter among the ramekins, being careful to seal in the sauce.
5 Place the ramekins directly into the air fryer basket, and bake for 16–18 minutes until the cake is golden and firm, but with a slight wobble.
6 Let cool for a few minutes before flipping out onto plates. Serve with salted caramel ice cream.

**Prep + cook time
50 minutes
Makes 4**

BANANA GALETTE
WITH CHOCOLATE FUDGE SAUCE

½ cup (120g) butter, softened
½ cup (80g) powdered sugar
1 egg, beaten
½ tsp vanilla extract
½ tsp salt
1½ cups (200g) all-purpose flour,
    plus extra for dusting
3 small ripe bananas, peeled
1 egg, beaten
to serve: ice cream

FRANGIPANE:
4 tbsp (50g) butter, softened
¼ cup (50g) sugar
¾ cup (80g) ground hazelnuts
1 egg
2 tbsp unsweetened cocoa powder
2 tbsp all-purpose flour

SAUCE:
1 x 14oz (400g) can sweetened
    condensed milk
1½ tbsp (20g) butter
3½oz (100g) dark chocolate
2 tbsp unsweetened cocoa powder,
    plus extra to serve
1 tsp vanilla extract

1 Combine the butter with the powdered sugar in a mixing bowl and beat until light. Stir in the beaten egg, vanilla, and salt, then fold in the flour until you have a stiff dough.
2 Form the dough into a ball and flatten into a 1in (2.5cm) thick disc, wrap in plastic wrap, and chill for 30 minutes in the fridge.
3 Meanwhile, make the frangipane. Combine the butter, sugar, and hazelnuts in a bowl. Beat in the egg, then sift in the cocoa and flour. Fold through until combined.
4 On a floured surface, roll out the pastry into a 12in (30cm) circle. Place on a parchment paper–lined baking sheet.
5 Spread the frangipane in the center of the circle, leaving a 2in (5cm) border around the edge. Halve the bananas lengthwise and place on the frangipane, pushing them in so the frangipane comes up around the fruit.

6 Fold the edges of the pastry into the center, cover in plastic wrap, and place in the fridge to chill for at least 30 minutes (and up to overnight).
7 Once chilled, brush the edges of the pastry with beaten egg. Trim any excess parchment paper so you have just enough to be able to lift the tart in and out of the basket.
8 Preheat the air fryer to 350°F for 3 minutes.
9 Place in the air fryer basket and cook at 350°F for 35 minutes.
10 Meanwhile, combine all the sauce ingredients in a small pan over low heat and stir until melted.
11 Let the galette cool in the basket for 20 minutes, before sliding out. Serve with the warm chocolate sauce, ice cream, and a dusting of cocoa powder.

**Prep + cook time
1 hour 30 minutes,
plus chilling
Serves 8**

CHERRY & RICOTTA CRUMBLE

1lb (450g) frozen cherries
¾ cup (150g) sugar
juice of 1 lemon
2 tbsp brandy or liquor of choice (optional)
3 tsp cornstarch
½ cup (100g) ricotta
to serve: store-bought custard

CRUMBLE:
4 tbsp (60g) butter, cubed and cold
¾ cup (100g) whole wheat flour
¼ cup (50g) light brown sugar
⅓ cup (50g) hazelnuts, roughly chopped
1 tsp flaked sea salt

1 Preheat the air fryer to 350°F for 3 minutes.
2 Combine the cherries, sugar, lemon juice, brandy (if using), and cornstarch in a bowl, stirring until the cornstarch has dissolved. Pour into a 8in (20cm) heatproof dish.
3 Bake at 350°F for 20 minutes, stirring halfway through. If the cherry filling is liquidy, place back in the air fryer at 400°F for 5 minutes (this will help activate the cornstarch).
4 Meanwhile, make the crumble. Place the cold cubed butter and flour in a mixing bowl, and, using your fingertips, rub the butter into the flour until it resembles coarse sand. Stir in the sugar, hazelnuts, and salt.

5 Remove the heatproof dish from the air fryer, dollop the ricotta all over using a small spoon, then cover the top with the crumble. Place back in the air fryer basket and bake for a further 25 minutes at 350°F, or until the crumble is golden and the filling is bubbling up through the edges.
6 Let cool for 10–15 minutes before serving with custard.

KEEP IT This will keep for up to 3 days in an airtight container in the fridge.

Prep + cook time
1 hour 30 minutes
Serves 6

RHUBARB & GINGER COBBLER

1lb 5oz (600g) rhubarb
2¼oz (65g) candied ginger in syrup, chopped, plus 2 tbsp of the syrup
½ cup plus 2 tbsp (125g) light brown sugar
grated zest and juice of 1 lemon
1½ tsp cornstarch
to serve: custard

COBBLER TOPPING:
5 tbsp (80g) butter, softened
⅓ cup (70g) sugar
1 cup (125g) all-purpose flour
½ tsp salt
½ tsp baking powder
¼ cup (60ml) milk
1 tsp vanilla extract

1 Preheat the air fryer to 350°F for 3 minutes.
2 Trim the rhubarb and cut into 1in (2.5cm) chunks. Combine in a mixing bowl with the chopped ginger, sugar, lemon juice and zest, and cornstarch. Give the mixture a good stir, then pour into a 9in (22cm) heatproof dish.
3 Roast for 15 minutes at 350°F, stirring every 5 minutes.
4 Meanwhile, make the cobbler topping. Combine the butter and sugar in a large mixing bowl and beat for 2 minutes, then add all the remaining ingredients and mix until you have a smooth but thick batter.
5 Remove the filling from the air fryer and add the cobbler topping.

6 Place straight back in the air fryer to bake for 18–20 minutes, or until the top is golden and the filling is bubbling through the gaps.
7 Let cool for 10 minutes before serving with custard.

KEEP IT Will keep for up to 5 days in an airtight container in the fridge.

Prep + cook time
50 minutes
Serves 4–6

MINI MERINGUE SUNDAES

⅔ cup (150ml) heavy cream
1 tsp vanilla extract
3½oz (100g) raspberries
4–6 scoops of raspberry sorbet
pulp of 2 passion fruits
4–6 tbsp white chocolate sauce
2–4 tbsp chopped nuts

MERINGUE:
2 egg whites
½ tsp white wine vinegar
½ tsp cornstarch
½ cup plus 2 tbsp (120g) sugar
2–3 drops pink food coloring
   (optional)

1 Start by making the meringue. Place the egg whites in a large mixing bowl. Using a handheld electric mixer, mix the egg whites on medium speed until frothy and doubled in size. Add the white wine vinegar and cornstarch, and mix for 30 seconds. Now, gradually add the sugar, a spoon at a time. Keep mixing until all the sugar is combined and the mixture is thick and glossy. Mix in the food coloring, if using.

2 Preheat the air fryer to 250°F for 3 minutes.

3 Cut a piece of parchment paper to fit the air fryer basket. Use a little dab of meringue to stick each corner of the paper down to the basket. Using a teaspoon, place dollops of meringue into the basket. They will puff up and double in size, so leave a 1in (2.5cm) gap between them.

4 Bake at 250°F for 20 minutes, in batches, until all the meringue is used. Let cool on a wire rack.

5 To assemble the sundaes, whip the cream with the vanilla extract to soft peaks. In sundae glasses, layer the whipped cream, meringues, berries, and a scoop of sorbet, then top with more cream, berries, and meringue. Finish with passion fruit pulp, chocolate sauce, and chopped nuts.

KEEP IT Extra meringues can be kept in an airtight container for up to 5 days.

**Prep + cook time
1 hour
Makes 4–6
(24 mini meringues)**

CHOCOLATE PAVLOVA

1¼ cups (300ml) heavy cream
1 tbsp icing powdered sugar
1 tsp vanilla extract
4 tbsp salted caramel sauce
to decorate: dark, milk, and white
   chocolate candy and chocolate
   covered pretzels

MERINGUE:
4 egg whites
1 tsp white wine vinegar
1 tsp cornstarch
1¼ cups (240g) sugar
2 tbsp unsweetened cocoa powder

1 Start by making the meringue. Place the egg whites in a large mixing bowl. Using a handheld electric mixer, mix the egg whites on medium speed until frothy and doubled in size. Add the white wine vinegar and cornstarch, and mix again for 30 seconds. Gradually add the sugar, a spoon at a time. Keep mixing until all the sugar is combined and the mixture is thick and glossy.
2 Put half of the meringue in another bowl and sift in the cocoa powder. Fold through gently—it doesn't need to be fully combined, just swirled.
3 In a parchment paper-lined 8in (20cm) loose-bottomed round pan, alternate spoonfuls of plain meringue and cocoa meringue. Using a spoon, swirl the mixes together. Using the back of a spoon, create a dip in the center for the cream and toppings to sit once baked.

4 Preheat the air fryer to 50°F for 3 minutes.
5 Place the pavlova in the preheated air fryer basket and bake at 250°F for 40 minutes, then turn down the temperature to 200°F and bake for a further 30 minutes.
6 Let the meringue cool completely in the pan on a wire rack before gently removing it from the pan and placing it on a serving plate.
7 Whip the cream with the powdered sugar and vanilla to soft peaks, then spoon over the center of the pavlova. Drizzle on the salted caramel and arrange the chocolates on top, and serve!

KEEP IT Will keep in the fridge for up to 3 days in an airtight container.

Prep + cook time
2 hours
Serves 6–8

PINEAPPLE FRITTERS WITH RUM CARAMEL SAUCE

½ cup (50g) cornstarch
½ cup (70g) all-purpose flour
½ cup (35g) shredded dried coconut
½ cup (120ml) sparkling water
2 tbsp sugar
1 pineapple, trimmed and cut
 into batons
vegetable oil cooking spray
to serve: toasted coconut

RUM CARAMEL SAUCE:
1 cup (200g) sugar
3 tbsp water
½ cup (120ml) heavy cream
3 tbsp (40g) butter
2 tbsp rum
1 tsp flaked sea salt

1 First, make the rum caramel sauce. Place the sugar in a wide heavy-based pan and add the water around the edge of the pan. Place on medium heat and, as the sugar starts to melt, swirl the pan. Do not stir the sugar, as it can cause sugar crystals to form resulting in a lumpy caramel. Keep swirling the pan until the sugar turns a deep golden brown; it will be bubbling and starting to gently smoke.

2 Turn off the heat and pour the cream into the pan, being careful as the caramel will bubble and spit. Once the mixture has calmed slightly, swirl the pan again, then add the butter, rum, and sea salt. Use a whisk to combine. Let the caramel cool in the pan for 10–15 minutes before pouring into a heatproof container. Set aside.

3 In a mixing bowl, add the cornstarch, flour, shredded coconut, sparkling water, and sugar and whisk until all the flour is absorbed.

4 Preheat the air fryer to 400°F for 3 minutes and line an air fryer basket with parchment paper.

5 Toss chunks of pineapple in the batter to coat on all sides. Using tongs, lift the slices of pineapple into the parchment paper–lined air fryer basket, leaving 2in (5cm) between each piece.

6 Bake at 400°F for 8 minutes, then spray with oil and bake for a further 2–4 minutes until starting to golden.

7 Remove the fritters from the basket and coat in the rum caramel.

8 Place on a serving platter, sprinkle with toasted coconut, and serve with extra caramel sauce.

**Prep + cook time
45 minutes
Serves 6**

BAKED PEACHES

4 firm-but-ripe peaches, pitted and
  halved
juice of 1 lemon
1 tsp vanilla extract
2 tbsp sugar
to serve: custard

CRUMBLE TOP:
2 tbsp (30g) butter, cold and cubed
½ cup) all-purpose flour
2½ tbsp (30g) raw sugar
¼ cup (20g) slivered almonds
1 tsp flaked sea salt

1 Preheat the air fryer to 350°F for 3 minutes.
2 Place the halved peaches in a 8in (20cm) heatproof dish, cut-side up, and squeeze over the lemon juice. Add the vanilla and sugar, and mix to coat. Place in the air fryer basket and bake for 5 minutes at 350°F.
3 To make the crumble, place the cold cubed butter in a small bowl with the flour, and rub the butter into the flour using your fingertips until it resembles coarse sand. Stir in the sugar, almonds, and sea salt.
4 Cover the peaches with mounds of the crumble (don't worry if it falls off the peaches into the dish, these bits will caramelize and can be scooped out).

5 Bake for a further 10 minutes at 350°F, or until the crumble is golden and the peaches are soft.
6 Serve warm with custard and any bits of crumble from the air fryer basket.

KEEP IT Can be kept for up to 5 days in an airtight container in the fridge.

Prep + cook time
30 minutes
Serves 4

VANILLA RICE PUDDING

½ cup (100g) jasmine rice
2 cups (500ml) milk
5 tbsp (60g) light brown sugar
1 tsp vanilla extract
½ tsp fine salt
1 cup (200ml) heavy cream
to serve: raspberry jam,
    nut butter, and cream

1 Preheat the air fryer to 325°F for 3 minutes.
2 Combine the rice, milk, brown sugar, vanilla, and salt in an 8in (20cm) heatproof dish.
3 Place in the air fryer basket and bake at 325°F for 30 minutes, stirring every 10 minutes to ensure even cooking. The rice should be tender but still have a little bite to it; taste the rice at each 10-minute interval and amend the cooking time to suit your preferred level of bite.

4 Once the rice is cooked, all the milk has been absorbed, and it has a silky consistency, remove the dish from the air fryer and stir in the cream.
5 Serve warm with raspberry jam, nut butter, and cream.

KEEP IT Can be chilled and eaten cold. Keep for up to 3 days in an airtight container.

Prep + cook time
45 minutes
Serves 2–4

APPLE HOT CROSS BUN PUDDING

⅔ cup (150ml) milk
⅓ cup (75ml) heavy cream
¼ cup (60g) cane sugar
1 tsp vanilla extract
1 egg
4 premade hot cross buns
3½ tbsp (50g) butter
2 tbsp raw sugar

FILLING:
3 firm apples, such as cosmic crisp
    or pink lady, peeled, cored, and
    chopped into ½in pieces
⅓ cup (50g) golden raisins
2½ tbsp (30g) cane sugar
1½ tbsp (20g) butter
juice of ½ lemon
1 tsp ground cinnamon

1 Preheat the air fryer to 325°F for 3 minutes.
2 Start by making the filling. Combine the chopped apples with the raisins, sugar, butter, and lemon juice in an 8in (20cm) round heatproof dish.
3 Place in the air fryer and bake for 15 minutes at 325°F, checking at 5-minute intervals and giving the apples a good mix each time. Once baked, set aside to cool.
4 In a large mixing bowl, add the milk and cream, and combine with the sugar, vanilla, and egg. Whisk thoroughly until you have a smooth custard-like liquid.
5 Cut the hot cross buns in half, and butter generously. Place one piece of bun in the ovenproof dish, followed by a spoonful of the apple filling and repeat until all the mix is used.

6 Pour the custard mix gently all over (you may need to wait for it to soak in a little before pouring it all in). You can use the back of a spoon to press down the buns to help make space for all the filling.
7 Preheat the air fryer to 350°F for 3 minutes.
8 Sprinkle the top of the pudding with the raw sugar, then place in the air fryer and cook at 350°F for 25 minutes until puffed up with a deep golden crust.

SERVE IT Serve warm with cream or a scoop of ice cream.

KEEP IT Can be kept for up to 3 days in an airtight container in the fridge.

Prep + cook time
1 hour
Serves 6

DUTCH BABY WITH BLUEBERRY COMPOTE

½ cup (70g) all-purpose flour
½ tsp salt
¼ tsp baking powder
2 tsp sugar
⅓ cup (80ml) milk
2 eggs, beaten
½ tsp vanilla extract
4 tsp (20ml) vegetable oil
to serve: ice cream and powdered
   sugar

BLUEBERRY COMPOTE:
1½ cups (200g) blueberries
¼ cup (50g) sugar
grated zest and juice of 1 lemon

1 Place the flour, salt, baking powder, and sugar in a mixing bowl. Make a well in the middle, then add the milk, eggs, and vanilla, and whisk until smooth. Set aside for 20 minutes to rest.

2 Preheat the air fryer to 350°F for 3 minutes.

3 Put all the blueberry compote ingredients in a heatproof dish and place in the air fryer for 10 minutes at 350°F. Remove and set aside.

4 Increase the temperature to 400°F.

5 Put the vegetable oil in a 7in (18cm) round cake pan, and heat in the air fryer at 400°F for 3 minutes. The oil needs to be smoking hot, so be careful and do not try to lift the dish out of the basket at this point.

6 Pour the batter directly into the hot oil, then bake for 12 minutes at 400°F.

7 Using tongs, lift the (now inflated) Dutch baby and flip it upside down, then bake for a further 8 minutes to crisp the bottom.

8 Serve immediately while hot, topped with the blueberry compote and ice cream and dusted with powdered sugar.

**Prep + cook time
50 minutes
Serves 4–6**

CONVERSION CHART

DRY MEASURES

metric	imperial
15g	½oz
30g	1oz
60g	2oz
90g	3oz
125g	4oz (¼lb)
155g	5oz
185g	6oz
220g	7oz
250g	8oz (½lb)
280g	9oz
315g	10oz
345g	11oz
375g	12oz (¾lb)
410g	13oz
440g	14oz
470g	15oz
500g	16oz (1lb)
750g	24oz (1½lb)
1kg	32oz (2lb)

OVEN TEMPERATURES

The oven temperatures below are for conventional ovens; if you are using a fan-forced oven, reduce the temperature by 20 degrees.

	°C (Celsius)	°F (Fahrenheit)
Very slow	120	250
Slow	150	300
Moderately slow	160	325
Moderate	180	350
Moderately hot	200	400
Hot	220	425
Very hot	240	475

One Australian metric tablespoon holds 20ml; one Australian metric teaspoon holds 5ml. North America, New Zealand and the United Kingdom use a 15ml tablespoon. The most accurate way of measuring dry ingredients is to weigh them.

LIQUID MEASURES

metric	imperial
30ml	1 fluid oz
60ml	2 fluid oz
100ml	3 fluid oz
125ml	4 fluid oz
150ml	5 fluid oz
190ml	6 fluid oz
250ml	8 fluid oz
300ml	10 fluid oz
500ml	16 fluid oz
600ml	20 fluid oz
1,000ml (1 liter)	1 quart

LENGTH MEASURES

metric	imperial
3mm	⅛in
6mm	¼in
1cm	½in
2cm	¾in
2.5cm	1in
5cm	2in
6cm	2½in
8cm	3in
10cm	4in
13cm	5in
15cm	6in
18cm	7in
20cm	8in
22cm	9in
25cm	10in
28cm	11in
30cm	12in (1ft)

INDEX